Einar M. Skaalvik
and Liv Finbak

Adult education in Great Britain, Norway and Spain

A comparative study of participation, motivation and barriers

Report from the Leonardo da Vinci Supported "MOBA" project

© Tapir Academic Press, Trondheim 2001

ISBN 82-519-1669-0

This publication may not be reproduced, stored in a retrieval system or transmitted in any form or by any means; electronic, electrostatic, magnetic tape, mechanical, photo-copying, recording or otherwise, without permission.

Printed by Tapir Trykkeri
Binding: Tapir Trykkeri

Partners:
Fundación Formación y Empleo (FOREM) in Spain
Statistics Norway (SN) in Norway
The Norwegian Institute for Adult Education (VOX) (formerly NVI) in Norway
The National Institute of Adult Continuing Education (NIACE) in England and Wales

Tapir Academic Press
N–7005 TRONDHEIM

Tel.:   + 47 73 59 32 10
Fax: + 47 73 59 32 04
E-mail: forlag@tapir.no
http://www.tapir.no/forlag

PREFACE

The purpose of the MOBA-project (Motivation for and barriers against participation in adult education) is to survey the participation of adults in education and training in Great Britain, Norway, and Spain, and to obtain a better understanding of psychological processes underlying participation and non-participation in such education. The research examines both the overall scale of participation and participation in different types of courses. It also explores differences between groups of respondents with respect to participation. Furthermore, the project focuses on motives for actual participation, plans and wishes of future participation as well as factors that prevent participation. We have also examined the relation between participation and different psychological variables, for instance self-confidence, intrinsic motivation for learning, perceived need for learning, and preferred strategies for learning.

The rapid development and the increased competition in the labour market make continuing education a necessity for an increasing number of people. Previous Norwegian surveys have also shown that an increasing part of adult education is work related. Equal opportunities for adults to engage in education are therefore important in order to combat exclusion from the labour market. In order to provide more equal opportunities for engagement in education we need to understand the psychological processes involved in participation in education.

The survey is organised as a co-operative project involving FOREM[1] in Spain, NIACE[2] in Great Britain and VOX[3] and SN[4] in Norway. The Norwegian Institute for Adult Education has acted as the co-ordinator for the work of the project, in addition to being responsible for the Norwegian part of the project. Professor Einar Skaalvik has been project manager. The project group has consisted of Carmen Cardenas and Rosa Maria Espino at FOREM, Liv Finbak, Ole H. Ljosland, and Einar M. Skaalvik at VOX and Naomi E. Sargant at NIACE. Margaret Crosbie at NIACE and Margit Myklebust at VOX have handled all the administrative challenges.

The MOBA project is financed by the EC Leonardo da Vinci programme, and by contributions from the various partners. Each of the partners has previously published national reports.[5]

This report has the following structure. Chapter 1 covers some central concepts and shows how these are defined in the MOBA survey. Chapter 2 reports results from previous surveys, whereas chapter 3 is devoted to theories related to participation, motivation and barriers. Chapter 4 presents the methods that were used to collect and analyse the data as well as a

---

[1] FOREM: Fundación Formación y Empleo.
[2] NIACE: National Institute of Adult Continuing Education.
[3] VOX: The Norwegian Institute for Adult Education (former NVI: Norwegian Institute of Adult Education).
[4] SN: Statistics Norway.
[5] Motivaciones y varreras para la perticipatión en la education de adults. Madrid, FOREM 2000.
Sargant, N. (2000). Motivation for and barriers to participation in adult learning - a study across Norway, Spain and Great Britain. England, NIACE.
Skaalvik, E.M., Finbak, L, & Ljosland, O.H. (2000). Voksenopplæring i Norge ved tusenårsskiftet. Deltakelse, motivasjon og barrierer. Trondheim, Norsk voksenpedagogisk forskningsinstitutt.

brief description of the samples. Chapters 5-9 present the results of the surveys whereas chapter 10 offers a summary and a discussion of the results.

CONTENT

1 CLARIFICATION OF TERMS --- 1
   1.1   Adult education as organised learning --- 1
   1.2   Compulsory schooling and ordinary studies ------------------------------------ 1
   1.3   Length of courses -- 2
   1.4   Formal competence or not? --- 2
   1.5   Different categories of courses --- 2
   1.6   Clarification of other terms -- 2

2 PREVIOUS PARTICIPATION SURVEYS -- 4
   2.1   Gender differences --- 4
   2.2   Age and participation -- 4
   2.3   Level of education and participation -- 4
   2.4   Occupation and participation in adult learning -------------------------------- 5
   2.5   The desire for more training --- 5

3 THEORETICAL PERSPECTIVES ON PARTICIPATION IN ADULT EDUCATION --------- 6
   3.1   Motives for participation in adult education ---------------------------------- 6
   3.2   Cognitive and affective variables that are associated with participation --------- 8
      3.2.1   Self-perception --- 8
      3.2.2   Perceived value of learning --- 9
   3.3   Barriers to participation --- 9

4 METHODOLOGY --- 11
   4.1   Samples --- 11
   4.2   The interview --- 11
   4.3   Sources of error --- 12
   4.4   Analysis --- 12
   4.5   Description of the three samples --- 13
      4.5.1   Gender and age --- 14
      4.5.2   Level of education and employment status ----------------------------- 14
      4.5.3   City size --- 14
      4.5.4   Size of household -- 14
      4.5.5   Access to telephone, computer and Internet ----------------------------- 14

5 PARTICIPATION IN ADULT EDUCATION -- 15
   5.1   The scale of participation --- 15
      5.1.1   Overall participation --- 15
      5.1.2   Participation in different types of course -------------------------------- 15
      5.1.3   Number of courses in the three-year period ----------------------------- 16
   5.2   Who takes part in courses? --- 17
      5.2.1   Gender -- 18
      5.2.2   Age --- 19
      5.2.3   Level of education -- 19
      5.2.4   Employment status -- 20
   5.3   A picture of adult education: description of the most recent course ----------- 20
      5.3.1   Course providers -- 21
      5.3.2   Duration of course -- 22
      5.3.3   Weekly time consumption --- 23
      5.3.4   Participation during work hours and paid leave ------------------------- 23
   5.4   Self-confidence and perceived value of learning ----------------------------- 23

6 MOTIVATION FOR PARTICIPATION -- 27
   6.1   Reasons for participation --- 27
      6.1.1   The most important reasons for participating on courses ----------------- 27
      6.1.2   Categories of reasons --- 28
      6.1.3   The importance of each category --------------------------------------- 29
   6.2   Intention to participate in future learning ----------------------------------- 30

	6.2.1	Likelihood of starting a course in the next three years	30
	6.2.2	Variables predicting likelihood of starting a course in the next three years	32
	6.2.3	Opportunities and desire for courses in working hours	33

7 BENEFITS OF ADULT EDUCATION ... 36
7.1 Categories of benefit ... 36
7.2 Judgement of benefit in the three countries ... 36
7.3 Benefits for different groups of participants ... 38

8 BARRIERS TO PARTICIPATION ... 40
8.1 Reasons for not participating in courses ... 40
8.2 Categories of barriers ... 41
8.3 The relative importance of the categories ... 42
8.4 Barriers in subgroups ... 43
8.5 Comments ... 45

9 ADULTS' LEARNING STRATEGIES ... 48
9.1 Choosing learning subjects ... 48
9.2 Self-evaluation of prior knowledge ... 48
9.3 Preferred learning strategies ... 48
9.4 The significance of prior knowledge in the choice of learning strategies ... 50
9.5 Strategies in different subgroups ... 51
9.6 Comments ... 51

10 SUMMARY AND DISCUSSION ... 53
10.1 The scale of adult education and description of the courses ... 53
10.2 Who takes part in adult education? ... 53
10.3 Motivation for participation ... 54
10.4 Benefits of adult education ... 55
10.5 Barriers ... 56
10.6 Adults' learning strategies ... 57
10.7 A model for participation in adult education ... 57

REFERENCES ... 61
LIST OF FIGURES ... 65
LIST OF TABLES ... 65
APPENDIX ... 67

1 CLARIFICATION OF TERMS

The term *adult education* is not clear and can be defined in different ways. One encounters a number of dilemmas when trying to define this term. When does a person become an adult? Should full-time study and compulsory schooling be categorised as adult education when the participants are above a certain age? What about informal learning which takes part in the work-place? Is it adult education when someone needs new knowledge and goes to different sources to learn on his own? Or should the term be narrowed down to cover only training that produces formal competence?

1.1 Adult education as organised learning

Jonstone & Rivera (1965) emphasise two criteria that must be fulfilled if a learning activity should be classified as adult education. Firstly, the main aim of the activity must be to acquire knowledge, information or skills. Secondly, the activity must be organised around one or another form of instruction.

In this survey, we have limited the term adult education to *organised* learning, even though a great deal of non-organised and informal learning goes on amongst adults. By organised learning we mean that some degree of supervision or instruction is associated with the learning situation. However, the *arena* for education is not decisive. This means, for example, that organised distance learning with home computers comes under our definition. The same is true of training and competence raising in the work place, as long as it is connected with some degree of teaching, instruction or supervision.

1.2 Compulsory schooling and ordinary studies

If we define all learning amongst people over 18 years of age as adult education, we encounter another problem. A large proportion of young people between 18 and 19 years of age are still at school and many are full-time students until well into their twenties. Traditionally, normal schooling and first-time education have not been regarded as adult education. Cross (1981) for example, refers to the following definition which the National Center of Education Statistics has used in the USA:

Adult education consists of courses and other educational activities, organised by teacher or sponsoring agency, and taken by persons beyond compulsory school age. Excluded is full-time attendance in a program leading to a high school diploma or an academic degree.

Thus, Cross does not include pupils of compulsory school age or full-time students at high school or university in the group that falls within the adult education concept. The Norwegian term «folkehøgskole» however, shows that this form of schooling in Norway has been regarded as adult education when it does not form part of an on-going education, but is taken after a break in education. This illustrates the problem in limiting the term adult education.

In the present survey, we have defined *all organised learning by people over the age of 18* as adult education. This means that pupils and students over 18 years of age who are involved in first-time education will also be regarded as participants in adult education. It is important to take this into consideration when reading and interpreting the results. However, we have information about which respondents are pupils and students and, where necessary, will check whether the results deviate if we ignore these participants. This group comprises a total of 5.6 % of the net sample.

1.3 Length of courses

Using the definition outlined above, all courses are registered irrelevant of their duration. A one-year full-time course and a two-hour course will therefore be registered as single courses in this context. School and studies that involve several subjects or topics will be treated as one course. This was made clear in the instructions given by the interviewers.

1.4 Formal competence or not?

Only some of the courses that are offered within working life or during leisure time result in *formal competence* of any kind. In this survey, we regard both courses which result in formal competence or certification, and courses that do not as adult education.

1.5 Different categories of courses

Adult education was in this project classified in four categories: general courses, work-related courses, hobby and leisure time courses and other courses. We have given the following clarifications of these terms:

General and academic courses are courses which are not directed towards a given occupation and which are not connected with recreation or leisure.

Vocational and work-related courses are courses that the respondents feel are related to their current or future work.

Recreational and leisure courses are courses connected to recreation or spare-time activities, and which the respondents themselves define as being related to their spare-time activities.

Other courses are courses which do not fall into any of the above categories.

1.6 Clarification of other terms

Respondents are regarded as being *employed* if they have a minimum working time of 10 hours per week on average. *Students* must be at school or studying as their main activity for at least 10 hours a week in order to be included in the student category. In order to be included in the category of the *unemployed,* the respondent must have been out of work for at least three months. *Not seeking work* means those who are not in paid work and are not seeking paid work.

Adult education centres are defined as institutions that are set up by the state or the local authorities with the purpose of offering adult education. *Private providers* are, for example, commercial firms or institutions that offer training or courses in different areas and which offer their services to companies, public departments and individuals. Study organisations also come into this category. *Voluntary organisations* are for example, membership organisations such as environmental organisations, religious and charitable organisations and other organisations that run courses within their own areas of interest.

2 PREVIOUS PARTICIPATION SURVEYS

Several surveys on participation in adult education have been carried out in Great Britain and Norway over the last 20 years (e.g., Sargant, 1991; Sargant et al. 1997; Skaalvik & Knudsen, 1979; Skaalvik & Engesbak, 1996; Tuckett & Sargant, 1999 - see also a review of British surveys by Hillage et al., 2000), whereas we are aware of only one Spanish survey focussing on academic adult education (AREA, 1984 - personal communication with Carmen Cardenas). A recent OECD report also survey adult education in 29 OECD countries (OECD, 1998). Some results from these surveys are described below.

2.1 Gender differences

The results of the surveys are inconsistent with respect to differences in participation among men and women. The Spanish survey, focusing on academic adult education showed that women participated slightly more frequently than men. Both the British and the Norwegian surveys showed that men took part in work-related courses more than women, while women participated more than men in other types of courses. A possible explanation of this may be that men are more oriented towards career development, while women may be more motivated towards general self-development when they engage in courses. In the course of the period between the two Norwegian surveys, however, the difference between men and women evened out regarding their participation in work-related courses.

2.2 Age and participation

Surveys in all countries reveal that the frequency of participation decreased with increasing age. These results suggest that there is a strong link between learning and work (Hillage et al., 2000). Nonetheless, the results of the two Norwegian surveys showed a marked change from 1979 to 1996. The 1979 survey showed that participation decreased evenly from 40 –50-years of age. In the 1996 survey, the participation curve dropped steeply at around 60 years. In other words, the 1996 survey showed that participation remained at a higher level across the age groups than previously.

The Norwegian surveys also showed that engagement in adult education decreases with age both for work related courses and courses that were not work related, indicating that the link between learning and work may not fully explain the differences between age groups in participation.

2.3 Level of education and participation

The surveys consistently show that that participation in adult education increases with higher levels of education. In general, the surveys show that respondents with low levels of education undertake less education/training as adults than respondents with higher levels of education. For instance, Sargant et al. (1997) showed that of those who left school at 18, 59 % had participated or were participating whereas of those who left school before they were 16, only 20 % had participated. In the Norwegian surveys relation between level of education and participation is particularly evident of work-related courses. The strong relation between level of education and participation is also reflected in the recent OECD report on education (OECD, 1998). Adults with a university degree undertook on average double the amount of training compared to adults with secondary school education. Furthermore, those with secondary school education in turn took on average double the amount of training compared with those who had only an elementary level of education.

2.4 Occupation and participation in adult learning

Having a job increases an individual's opportunity to take courses. Sargant (2000) found that about half of those asked who were in full time employment had recently or currently been involved in educational activities, compared to 41 % of unemployed people, 30 % of those who were not working and 16 % of retired people. Similar results are found in Norway (Skaalvik & Engesbak, 1996).

2.5 The desire for more training

In the 1996 survey (Skaalvik & Engesbak 1996), 65.5 % of those questioned replied that they wanted more adult education, and 67.4 % replied that they would take advantage of study leave with pay, if such an opportunity arose. The replies showed the desire for more education right up to the over 60s age-group. However, the wishes reflected in the survey did not always correspond with actual participation. The lack of similarity between expressed motivation and actual participation was particularly great amongst younger respondents with low levels of education. Also, 77 % of those who wanted more education wanted it to be work-related. The expressed goals reflect the increased need and the strong emphasis on training within work-related courses, which has been noted already in the period from 1979 to 1996.

3 THEORETICAL PERSPECTIVES ON PARTICIPATION IN ADULT EDUCATION

Empirical research connected with adult learning has been strongly focused on participation, with the central questions concerning the provision of education and training for adults and who participates in which type of course. The research has been relatively poorly founded in theory. The theoretical frameworks most used are theories of motivation and barriers.

The research on motivation and obstacles to participation in adult education can be divided into different strands:
(1) To some extent, research has endeavoured to clarify different *reasons or motives* for adults participating in education. This research often focuses situation-based reasons, for example, the need for training connected with changes in one's working situation.
(2) Researchers have also analysed *cognitive and affective variables that are associated with participation*. Such psychological conditions can be seen as relatively stable characteristics that may promote or reduce participation in adult education. Examples may include adults' self-confidence or their perception of their own learning abilities.
(3) The research has also been directed towards *barriers to access learning,* which prevent participation in adult education. Some researchers have included cognitive and affective variables such as lack of motivation for participation and low self-confidence as barriers. Thus, the different strands of research are clearly overlapping.

3.1 Motives for participation in adult education

A number of surveys have been carried out in order to explore reasons or motives for participation. In carrying out such surveys, participants in adult education are often asked to judge the significance of a number of possible reasons for participation. In many surveys, the results are then analysed statistically, using factor analysis. This is a technique which is based on the assumption that behind a number of concrete reasons lies a limited number of general motivation factors. The purpose of factor analysis is to examine which and how many underlying motivation factors can be identified.

Surveys of this type have given varying results with regard to the number and type of factors. Nonetheless, the results have several common traits. This is illustrated in Table 1, which shows what factors were found in two surveys (Boshier, 1991; Beder and Valentine, 1990). The two surveys found 7 and 10 motivation factors, respectively. However, the table only shows the factors which are clearly identifiable. Six of the motivation factors in the two surveys have clear similarities:

- The desire for self-development or self-improvement, including the wish to learn, the need for independence and a desire for increased self-concept or self-esteem.

- Needs connected with family responsibilities, including the desire to become better parents and to be better able to help children with their schoolwork.

- Social contact, including the desire to meet other people and to break the pattern of everyday routine.

- Reading and writing are more limited motives for improving capabilities within these areas.

- Career development includes different desires connected with jobs, from obtaining a job or changing jobs to making a career within the job one has and being better able to carry out this work.

- Educational preparation is used as an indication that participation in adult education is a preparation or qualification for subsequent education.

Table 1 Motivation factors identified in two surveys (Boshier, 1991; Beder and Valentine, 1990).

Factors found in the surveys		Terms used by Boshier, 1991	Terms used by Beder and Valentine, 1990
Factors found in both surveys	Self development	Cognitive interest	Self Improvement
	Family responsibilities	Family togetherness	Family responsibilities
	Social contact	Social contact	Diversion
	Reading and writing skills	Communication improvement	Literacy development
	Career development	Professional advancement	Job advancement
	Educational preparation	Educational preparation	Educational advancement
Factors found in only one survey	Community involvement		Community/ church involvement
	Economic need		Economic need
	Encouragement from others		Urging of others
	Something to do	Social stimulation	

A common feature for three of these motivation factors, career development, educational preparation, and family responsibilities, is that the respondents have clear goals which lie above and beyond the activity itself. Cross (1981) describes participants with these motives as «goal-oriented». Participants who have such motives take courses in order to achieve given goals, for example, learning to talk in front of a group or learning to tackle special family problems. Cross feels that goal-oriented persons first identify a *need* and subsequently look for learning opportunities. These types of motives have also been called "external motivation», while Boshier (1977) calls participants with such motives «life chance oriented».

One of the factors, self-development, has its goal to a large extent in the activity itself. This factor particularly concerns interest and the desire to learn. Cross calls this type of motivation «learning orientation». Terms such as intrinsic motivation (Deci and Ryan, 1985) and task-orientation (Nicholls, 1984) have also been used to describe this type of motivation.

The two remaining motivation factors which were found in both surveys, are not equally simple to classify. Participation in order to increase one's ability in reading and writing can partly be see as intrinsic motivation or task orientation, but there is also an identifiable need behind this goal, and participation clearly has a goal beyond the learning situation. Participation motivated by a desire for social contact and breaking out of the everyday routine is close to what Cross (1981) described as «activity orientation». Activity-oriented participants, according to Cross, participate more for the activity itself than in order to achieve specific learning goals. They may go on a course to avoid feelings of loneliness or boredom, or to get away from a job or home situation with which they are unhappy.

Norwegian surveys have previously shown that intrinsic motivation (interest in the subject) is the most important motive for participation in leisure-time courses, while career development is the most important motive for participation in work-related courses (Skaalvik, 1979). The most dominant career-related motive in Skaalvik's survey was being better able to carry to one's work. Skaalvik and Tvete (1980) also found that interest in the subject and self-improvement were the most important motives for participation.

In the MOBA project, we have focused on career–oriented motives, self-development, interest, social motives and educational preparation.

3.2 Cognitive and affective variables that are associated with participation

3.2.1 Self-perception

Previous research indicates that self-perception (self-confidence, perception of one's own learning abilities, level of competence, and expectations of being able to pass a course) are significantly related to participation in adult education (see Skaalvik and Knudsen, 1979).

Motivation researchers explain the relation between self-perception and participation in adult education in that self-perception has consequences both for motivation and behaviour. One explanation of this relation can be found in «self-efficacy» theory (Bandura, 1986; Pajares, 1997). Research connected with this tradition shows that people have a tendency to avoid situations and activities which require levels of competence which people do not believe they have. Efforts as well as perseverance in the face of difficulty and choices people make are affected by their self-efficacy. Those who have low expectations of their own competence will reduce their input more quickly or give up when they run into problems.

Participation in adult education is as a rule optional. Academic self-perception may therefore be of great significance for participation in learning activities once compulsory schooling is completed. This affects both recruitment for further and higher education and participation in adult education courses. Research into young people for example, has shown that academic self-perception is systematically related to both choice and completion of education (Hackett, 1995; Hackett, Betz, O'Halloran and Romac, 1990).

Covington (1992) gives another explanation of the relation between self-perception and motivation. He bases his theory on the fact that ability is highly valued in our society and that ability is seen as the most important cause of good or poor achievement. A positive perception of one's own abilities will therefore give a feeling of self worth. In an education situation, low expectation of one's ability to master a subject may result in a dilemma. On the one side, high effort will improve one's chances of doing well, while on the other hand, poor results, in spite of high input, may be seen as proof of low ability. Therefore, when perceptions of competency are low, input may appear threatening, which may arouse a need to defend self-perception. In this way, effort becomes a double-edged sword. Amongst school children, low mastery expectations may lead to decreased effort, as part of the defence of self-perception. Amongst adults who have a choice, low mastery expectations may lead them not to participate in education or to dropping out if mastery expectations are impaired.

In the MOBA-project, we have charted the respondents' self-confidence related to learning. One purpose of the analyses is to chart whether self-confidence is systematically related to adult participation in education.

3.2.2 Perceived value of learning

Believing that one can master a task is not a sufficient reason to engage in it. Nor is believing that one can complete a course in adult education sufficient to make one participate in it. Participation in a course must also have some kind of value for those who are attending it. This perspective is elaborated by Eccles (see Eccles, 1987; Eccles and Wigfield, 1989) in the «expectancy-value theory», where both expectations of competency and the value of the activity are seen as important preconditions for motivation. In this theory, the value of a task is expected to be positively correlated with expectations of mastery. Thus, expectations and values strengthen each other.

Wigfield and Eccles (1992) identify four different types of values: attainment value, intrinsic interest value, extrinsic utility value, and cost (see also Pintrich and Schunk, 1996). These types of values are related to the type of motivation that we discussed above. Extrinsic utility values are linked to the significance of the activity in achieving future goals. Participants whom Cross describes as goal oriented must therefore be assumed to emphasise extrinsic utility values of the education. Intrinsic interest value is described by Wigfield and Eccles as the enjoyment the pupils or participants obtain from working on a given task and is based on interest in the activity. This value focus is assumed to be strongest amongst those who are learning-oriented. Attainment value is connected to the participants' self-perception and competency expectations and implies that an activity unleashes largely positive feelings for those who feel they are mastering the activity. Costs are described by Eccles as all negative aspects involved with engaging oneself in a task, for example, all that has to be given up in order to engage oneself in a task. This is closely connected to barriers to learning.

In the research on adult participation in education, the value perspective has not been systematically analysed, but it has been studied indirectly through asking participants about their reasons for participating. In this project we have two measures of the value of learning or training; (a) intrinsic interest value or intrinsic motivation for learning, and (b) extrinsic utility value or expectation of outcome value of learning.

3.3 Barriers to participation

A number of surveys have been carried out to chart barriers to participation in adult education. In such surveys, the researchers must choose whether to classify lack of interest and low motivation as barriers. One possible consideration is that it is only meaningful to talk about barriers when people are motivated to learn. The question about barriers then becomes a question of what prevents those adults who are interested in learning from participating. Another possible consideration is that behind an expressed lack of interest may lie psychological barriers (see for example Rubenson, 1975). In this report, we have chosen to use the barrier concept in a broad perspective, as synonymous with reasons for not participating.

Researchers have classified barriers to participation different ways. Johnstone and Rivera (1965) distinguished broadly between external (environmental) obstacles and internal (psychological) obstacles. Cross (1981) distinguished between two types of external obstacles and categorised the obstacles in three main groups: *situational, institutional and dispositional* barriers. Situational barriers encompass matters such as costs, lack of time, care duties, responsibilities connected with work and transport. Institutional barriers involve study plans, lack of information, strict attendance requirements or the lack of a relevant course. Dispositional barriers include low self-confidence, lack of faith in one's learning ability, lack of desire or perseverance, and generally being tired of school.

Scanlan & Darkenwald (1984) studied a number of factors that hinder participation in education. By analysing a large number of variables, they found six main groups of barriers, both external and psychological. Darkenwald and Valentine (1985) labelled these factors in a later publication as follows:
1) Disengagement (inertia, apathy, negative attitudes);
2) Lack of quality (dissatisfaction with quality of available educational opportunities);
3) Cost;
4) Family constraints;
5) Lack of benefit (doubts about the worth and need for participation; and
6) Work constraints.

Skaalvik (1979) analysed the obstacles for adults who wanted to participate in adult education but who had not done so. External barriers were emphasised in this group, with lack of time as the most important, while psychological barriers such as a lack of self-confidence and a feeling of being too old were not emphasised by many respondents.

Researchers have also addressed the question of barriers more indirectly, by studying which groups within the population do not participate or participate least in adult education. Such studies have shown that participation is lowest amongst the following groups: the elderly, those who have the lowest levels of education and those who are unemployed (see for example Skaalvik, 1979; Skaalvik and Knudsen, 1979; Skaalvik and Engesbak, 1996). A particularly interesting question is whether these groups have different barriers to the groups which participate most, or whether it is simply a question of how strong these barriers are.

In the MOBA-project, we asked respondents who had not taken part in adult education during the last three years why they had not done so. In this context, we looked at both external barriers (e.g. lack of time, lack of courses, costs, travel routes and care obligations), lack of interest or need and (other) psychological barriers (e.g. lacking self-confidence and a feeling of being too old).

4 METHODOLOGY

4.1 Samples

In each country a representative sample of adults between the ages of 18 and 79 was asked if they were willing to participate in a personal interview. The sampling procedures are elaborated in previously published national reports (FOREM, 2000; Sargant, 2000; Skaalvik, Finbak & Ljosland, 2000). The net sample size in each country was 1571 in Great Britain, 1836 in Norway, and 1920 in Spain. The field work was carried out in the Autumn of 1999.

4.2 The interview

The information was obtained using a computer-aided structured interview (Appendix 1a). Trained interviewers were instructed to carry out the interview by visiting the respondents in person.

The major themes in the interview were:

- participation in adult education during the last three years
- reasons for participating
- reasons for not participating (barriers)
- practical considerations connected with the most recent course
- benefits of the most recent course
- future plans to participate in adult education
- reasons for participating in courses in the future
- evaluating own knowledge in different areas
- choice of learning strategy in different areas
- self-perception (in general and in relation to leaning)
- attitudes to learning
- work-place support for learning.

Amongst the background information obtained from all the respondents were: age, gender, education, personal income, family income, size of town, employment, weekly working hours, number of persons in household, and access to telephone, PC and the Internet.

The respondents were given the following explanation as an introduction to the interview:

> *I am now going to give you some questions about any education or training you have undertaken during the last three years. By education and training we mean formal education as well as any other short courses or educational activities which require some kind of instruction or supervision. This includes distance learning which you can do at home. For the rest of this section, we will refer to these as a course or courses. If you have been on an educational and training program which involved studying a number of subjects, please consider his as one course.*

General questions concerning self-perception, attitude to learning or future plans for training or courses were put to all those who participated in the interviews.

Questions concerning experiences of adults participating in education were only put to those who had taken courses in the three years prior to the interview. These questions were based on the *last course* which the respondent had completed. The questions were also put to those who had not completed their most recent course. The following information was given:

> *We shall now ask some questions about the last course that you have done, whether or not you have completed it. If you are doing a course at the moment, please count this course as the last one. If you are doing several courses at the moment, please choose the one you have done for the longest period of time.*

Questions regarding reasons for not taking courses (barriers) were only put to respondents who had not taken a course during the last three years.

The respondents themselves decided to which of the four given course categories (general courses, work-related courses, recreation or spare-time courses or other courses) their last course belonged. The interviewer was instructed to state our definitions (see Chapter 1 and Appendix 1b) if the respondent needed help in placing the courses in one of the four categories.

When the respondents were given a number of possible answers to choose between, a text was displayed on a card or a PC screen in addition to oral presentations, so that the respondent could see all the alternatives. These were listed on the card, so that the respondent could study them closely before he or she replied.

4.3 Sources of error

In common with many surveys into adult participation in education, this survey is based on self-reporting. The results therefore depend on how the respondents understood the explanations given by the interviewer. Some of the questions allowed for interpretation by the respondents. These include, for example, classification of courses as general, work-related or recreation or leisure courses.

The questionnaire (structured interview) was translated back and forth from Norwegian to English and back and forth from English to Spanish.

4.4 Analysis

Since the structure of the survey is quantitative, the analysis has been carried out according to normal statistical methods and the results are presented in tabular form with relevant comments. The background variables which are used throughout most of the tables are: age, gender, level of education and employment. Cross tabulations are used to show the relation between the background variables and variables which describe participation, attitudes towards participation, attitudes towards learning, self-perception, choice of learning strategy and motivation for further education.

The analyses in this report are based on unweighted data. Our report of the British results will therefore show some minor deviation compared to the national report, which was based on weighted data (see Sargant, 2000). These deviations, however, represents negligible details, whereas they do not affect the broad picture.

4.5 Description of the three samples

Differences between the three countries in participation in adult education may reflect basic differences between the samples. Table 2 therefore describe each sample with respect to key variables. For the British sample we present distributions based on both weighted and unweighted data. Our comments below are based on the unweighted data.

Table 2 Description of the samples. Percentages. Base = all respondents.

		Great Britain		Norway	Spain
		Weighted N=1571	Unweighted N=1571	Unweighted N=1836	Unweighted N=1920
Gender	Men	47	44	50	49
	Women	53	56	50	51
Age	18-29	19	16	24	27
	30-45	33	33	36	30
	46-59	25	24	23	21
	60-79	23	27	18	22
Level of education	No formal	32	34	0	17
	Primary school	23	24	16	53
	Upper secondary school	14	12	55	18
	College/university	24	23	28	12
	Other	8	8	2	1
Employment Status	Employed	61	57	70	44
	Unemployed	3	3	2	9
	Retired	18	21	17	18
	Not seeking work	14	15	3	22
	Student	2	1	6	9
	Other	3	3	2	0
City size	0-1999	14	13	31	4
	2000-19 999	20	20	24	30
	20 000-99 999	18	18	21	24
	100 000-199 000	11	11	6	9
	200 000-499 000	11	11	8	15
	> 500 000	27	28	10	20
Size of household (number of persons)	1	12	24	19	8
	2	37	37	32	23
	3	21	18	20	22
	4	19	15	18	28
	5 or more	11	7	11	18
Access telephone	No access	3	4	0	8
	Only at work	2	2	27	2
	Only at home	44	46	0	64
	Both at work and at home	48	45	72	23
	Other places	3	3	0	3
Access PC	No access	46	50	24	61
	Only at work	9	9	17	5
	Only at home	20	17	14	25
	Both at work and at home	24	22	45	9
	Other places	2	2	1	1
Access Internet	No access	34	35	42	86
	Only at work	17	18	16	6
	Only at home	24	23	19	5
	Both at work and at home	21	20	22	2
	Other places	4	4	1	2

4.5.1 Gender and age

The Norwegian and the Spanish sample had an equal distribution of men and women, whereas women were slightly overrepresented in the British data. Younger people are also slightly underrepresented and older people overrepresented in the British sample. It is important to bear this in mind when interpreting differences in overall scale of participation.

4.5.2 Level of education and employment status

There are important differences both with respect to level of education and employment status between the three countries. Norway has both the largest percentage of people with college and university education and the largest percentage of people with upper secondary education. In contrast, Great Britain and Spain have a much larger proportion of people with either primary school education or no formal education. A comparison of Great Britain and Spain also reveals that Great Britain has both a larger proportion of people with no formal education and college or university level of education.

In the three countries the employment rate is highest in Norway and lowest in Spain. There is also a large difference in the percentage of full time students in the three samples, with the highest percentage of students in Spain and the lowest in Great Britain. This difference calls for special attention in interpretations of results.

4.5.3 City size

Norway differs substantially from Great Britain and Spain in that a much larger proportion of the Norwegian population live in places with less than 2000 inhabitants, whereas the proportion of the population living in large cities is lower.

4.5.4 Size of household

The samples from Great Britain and Norway do not differ much with respect to the number of persons in the household. However, Spain differs from the two other samples in that the number of persons in the household is larger. Consequently, respondents from Spain may have greater difficulties finding time for attending adult education after working hours that respondents in Great Britain and Norway.

4.5.5 Access to telephone, computer and Internet

Access to telephone, computers, and Internet is interesting because it indicates both the level of technological knowhow and opportunity to use new technology in learning. The Norwegian population differ from Great Britain and Spain in that a larger proportion have access to telephone, both at home and at the workplace. The access to computers was also greatest in Norway where three out of four respondents confirmed such access. In comparison, fifty percent of the British respondents and forty percent of the Spanish respondents had access to computers. In Norway nearly half of the respondents had access to computers both at home and at the workplace, whereas this was true for only nine percent of the Spanish respondents. Also with respect to Internet the results revealed large differences between the samples. In Norway nearly six out of ten respondents had access to Internet, whereas thirtytwo percent of the British respondents and fourteen percent of the Spanish respondents had such access.

5 PARTICIPATION IN ADULT EDUCATION

5.1 The scale of participation

5.1.1 Overall participation

Table 3 shows the proportion of the respondents who were participating in adult education at the time of the interview, as well as the proportion who had participated in the course of the last three years. A comparison of the results shows some interesting tendencies. Participation at the time of the interviews varied little in the three countries. In the Norwegian sample, 17 % were taking part in adult education at that time. The corresponding figures in Spain and Great Britain were respectively 14 % and 16 %. However, the interviews in the three countries were carried out at different times during the course of autumn 1999, which makes the comparison uncertain.

The proportion of respondents in the three samples who had participated during the last three years, which is easier to compare, varied very strongly, however. Over the last three years, 70 % of the Norwegian sample had participated in adult education. Corresponding figures in Spain and Great Britain were respectively 32 % and 41 %. Thus, over a three-year period, which gives a better basis for comparison, it appears that the differences between the countries are very large.

When summarised, these results show that the volume of adult education at a given point in time, measured in the number of adults participating, is very similar in all three countries. Over a longer period, however, the proportion of adults who have participated in adult education is almost twice as high in Norway as in the other countries. This is partly due to the fact that the participation pattern is different in the three countries, with emphasis on different types of course and with a much greater proportion of short courses in Norway (see below).

Table 3 Participation in courses now and during the last 3 years. Percentages. Base = all respondents.

Participation	Great Britain N = 1571	Norway N = 1836	Spain N = 1920
Participates now	16	17	14
Participated during the last 3 years	41	70	32

5.1.2 Participation in different types of course

In order to obtain a more accurate picture of respondents' participation, we have distinguished between three categories of adult education. In the category of *general and academic courses* we have put courses which are of a general nature and which are neither directed towards a particular job / occupation nor connected with hobbies or leisure. *Vocational and work-related courses* are courses which the respondents feel are of relevance for current or future employment. *Recreation and leisure courses* are courses which are associated with recreation or leisure-time activities, and which the respondents themselves define as being connected with their own leisure time activities.

Table 4 gives an overview of the proportion of respondents who had participated in the different types of course. Many of the participants had taken part in two or more types of courses over the three-year period. The percentage of those who had participated in different types of courses in the last three years cannot therefore be summarised. In the course of the three-year period, 60 % of the respondents in the Norwegian sample had taken work-related courses, 13 % had taken general and academic courses, while 18 % had participated in recreation and leisure courses. The results show that adult education in Norway is dominated by work-related courses. A comparison with previous studies shows that it is within this area that the growth in adult education has been the greatest in recent years.

In Great Britain, work-related courses are also the type of course in which the majority has participated, but the difference in participation between the different types of course is less. Here, general and academic courses and recreation and leisure courses together have more or less the same proportion as work-related courses. The picture in Spain stands out most strongly against the picture in Norway. In Spain, the numbers taking general and academic courses and vocational and work-related course are virtually the same, respectively 15 % and 14 %. Adult education in Spain therefore appears to be more strongly focused on general academic education than is the case in Norway.

The results show that adult education has different content and different functions in the three countries. This reflects differences in the level of education, as shown in table 2.

Table 4 Percentage of all respondents who had participated in different kinds of courses during the last 3 years. Base =all respondents.

	Great Britain	Norway	Spain
	N = 1571	N = 1836	N = 1920
Participated in general and academic courses	14	13	15
Participated in vocational or work-related courses	29	60	14
Participated in recreational and leisure courses	9	18	5

Note: many participants had done more than one type of course during the period

5.1.3 Number of courses in the three-year period

In the current study, adult education is defined as all forms of organised teaching which contains some kind of instruction or supervision. No upper or lower limit for the duration or volume of teaching has been set. This means that the courses can vary from very short courses to more comprehensive learning and education. We will return to this in Chapter 6. Some participants may therefore have taken a number of short courses in the three-year period. In the study, the respondents who had participated in adult education were asked to state how many courses they had taken over the three-year period before the time of the interview.

Table 5 gives an overview of the number of courses taken by the participants in each type of course in the three-year period. When reading this table, it must be remembered that the base in each country in the table is the respondents had participated on one or more courses of the type in question .

The table shows differences in the participation pattern both between countries and between types of course. We found a general tendency for those who had participated in vocational and work-related courses to have participated in several courses in the course of the three years, while the majority of those who had participated in general and academic courses or recreational and leisure courses, had only taken one course. However, this tendency was clearest in Norway and Great Britain, where almost half of the participants on vocational and work-related courses had taken three courses or more.

By way of comparison, the tendency with general and academic courses and for recreational and leisure courses was that those who had taken such courses had, in the main, taken only one or two courses in the same period. Where general and academic courses are concerned, there is reason to believe that this type of education probably extends over longer periods and that schooling or studies which contain several subjects or topics were registered as one course.

Table 5 Percentage of participants who had taken 1, 2, 3, 4, 5 or 6 or more courses during the last 3 years. Base = all participants in each type of course.

Number of courses	General and academic courses			Vocational or work-related courses			Recreational and leisure courses		
	GB	Nor	Sp	GB	Nor	Sp	GB	Nor	Sp
	N= 214	N= 231	N= 292	N= 458	N= 1108	N= 262	N= 142	N= 334	N= 95
1	58	74	86	37	40	75	56	64	85
2	22	12	6	18	17	13	27	21	8
3	8	8	6	14	14	5	12	6	2
4	3	3	1	9	7	2	1	3	1
5	3	0	0	4	7	2	1	2	2
6 or more	5	4	1	18	15	2	4	4	1

As well as the fact that the majority of those who participate in adult education in Great Britain participate in vocational and work-related courses, it appears that it is very common to take several such courses. These results can further confirm the dominant place which vocational and work-related courses have within adult education in Norway and Great Britain. The increasing dominance of work-related courses reflects the need for readjustment in business life and this required adjustment leads to the individual workers increasing and renewing their competence. Once again the results from Spain show another picture and confirm that adult education in Spain is more strongly dominated by basic general learning. However there is every reason to believe that the development in Spain will follow the same patterns as we see in Norway and Great Britain.

5.2 Who takes part in courses?

Table 6 gives an overview of the total participation for all groups of respondents in the three countries, while table 7 shows the participation in different types of courses. Both the total participation and the participation distributed by course are considered in this chapter in relation to the respondents' gender, age, level of education, and employment status.

Table 6 Percentage participation in courses during the last 3 years. Base = all respondents in each category.

		Great Britain	Norway	Spain
Total		41	70	32
Gender:	Men	40	70	31
	Women	43	70	34
Age	18 – 29	64	88	64
	30 – 45	50	76	33
	46 – 59	42	73	18
	60 – 79	17	28	7
Level of Education:	No formal	18	**	7
	Primary /lower secondary school	45	40	27
	Upper secondary school	61	72	54
	College/university	65	83	60
Employment Status	Employed	55	80	37
	Unemployed	54	63*	43
	Retired	14	23	6
	Not seeking work	24	43	16
	Student	**	97	92

* Percentage must be interpreted with caution, due to low N (N ≥ 20 and < 30)
** N < 20

Table 7 Percentage participation in different types of courses during the last 3 years, grouped by gender, age, level of education and employment status. Base = all respondents in each category.

Categories of respondents	General and academic course			Vocational course			Recreational and leisure course		
	GB	Nor	Sp	GB	Nor	Sp	GB	Nor	Sp
Total	14	13	15	29	60	14	9	18	5
Gender									
Men	11	12	14	30	63	16	7	15	3
Women	16	13	17	28	58	12	11	22	7
Age									
18 – 29	35	30	47	43	76	17	8	29	5
30 – 45	16	9	7	40	70	21	9	17	6
46 – 59	6	7	3	32	65	12	10	14	3
60 – 97	5	3	1	5	16	1	10	12	5
Level of education									
No formal	3	**	1	10	**	3	5	**	3
Primary/lower sec.	11	10	11	32	26	11	7	13	5
Upper secondary	26	15	33	40	63	19	14	17	5
College/university	27	9	26	50	75	35	16	23	5
Employment status									
Employed	17	10	11	44	73	24	9	17	4
Unemployed	18	26*	19	38	48*	19	8	30*	3
Retired	5	3	1	2	9	1	10	12	5
Not seeking work	9	10	4	11	27	4	7	22	8
Student	**	56	87	**	77	8	**	40	8

* Percentage must be interpreted with caution, due to low N (N ≥ 20 and < 30)
** N < 20

5.2.1 Gender

Looking at the course categories as a whole, there are no major differences in men's and women's participation rates on courses (table 6). While participation was exactly the same for men and women in the Norwegian sample, we found small, but not significant differences between men's and women's participation in Great Britain and Spain. The results do not give any reason to claim that there are differences in participation between men and women in the three countries as long as the course categories are considered together.

When we look at men's and women's participation in different types of courses, we find that in all three countries a somewhat greater proportion of men has participated in vocational and work-related course courses compared to women. Here, the differences in participation for men and women are significant in Norway and Spain, but we do not find such differences in men's and women's participation in vocational and work-related courses in Great Britain. In both Great Britain and Spain, the proportion of women who have taken part in general and academic courses is significantly larger than the proportion of men, while in Norway there is not such a difference. However, a significantly larger proportion of women than men participate in recreational and leisure courses in all the three countries.

5.2.2 Age

Table 6 shows that participation alters with age. It shows that the youngest age group participates most, and that participation decreases gradually with increasing age. Nonetheless the picture is somewhat different in the three countries. In Spain, participation decreases evenly and dramatically with increasing age. The Norwegian sample is characterised by participation remaining at high and relatively stable level until around 60 years of age. In this period, participation decreases only weakly in the Norwegian sample. The British sample occupies a central position, with a gradual but not strong reduction in participation between 18 and 60 years of age.

This picture changes somewhat when we look at age in relation to participation on different types of courses (table 7). In all three countries, participation on general and academic courses drops steeply as early as the age of 30. This clarifies the general picture of participation in Spain, given that general and academic courses occupy such a dominant place in adult education in Spain. Where work-related courses are concerned, we find gradual but slowly decreasing participation until the age of 60 in Great Britain and Norway, while participation in vocational and work-related courses in Spain increases amongst the 30 to 45 age group, and then sinks towards pensionable age. In all the countries, therefore, we find that work-related courses maintain a relatively stable level until the end of working life. For recreational and leisure courses, participation is relatively even in all age groups in Great Britain and Spain, while the youngest age group in Norway participates relatively to the greatest extent in this type of course.

5.2.3 Level of education

The level of education of the respondents was divided into four categories: no formal education, primary / lower secondary school, upper secondary school, and college / university. As table 6 shows, there are very large differences in participation between groups with different levels of education in all three countries. Respondents with low levels of education participate to a relatively small extent in adult education, while participants with higher levels of education participate most. For all three countries there is a relatively dramatic increase in participation when the level of education of the respondents is above elementary school level.

The respondents' level of education also has an effect on participation in the different categories of courses (tables 7). In all the countries, we find a strong increase in participation on general and academic courses with increased levels of education up to upper secondary level. Thereafter, participation levels out in Great Britain, while it sinks in Norway and Spain. Where vocational and work-related courses are concerned, there is a clear increase in participation with the level of education in all three of the countries covered in this study. Here, participation is highest for those who have college- and university- level education. Nonetheless, there are still certain differences. In Great Britain, participation increases evenly with the level of education of the respondent. In Norway, we find the greatest difference between respondents who were educated to elementary school level and respondents who were educated above this level, while most important difference in Spain is between those who have university-level education and those who are educated below this level. In Great Britain and Norway, there is also an increasing tendency with the level of education towards participation in recreational and leisure courses, while participation on such courses in Spain appears to be more independent of the level of education. This can probably be explained by differences in working hours in the three countries. In Spain, in particular, where the working day is divided up by a long break and finishes relatively late, there may be less time for participation in other courses than for those who have pragmatic reasons.

5.2.4 Employment status

In table 6, we have divided the sample into five groups based on the respondents' employment status: students, employed, unemployed, retired, and respondents who are not seeking work. We can see from table 6 that the percentage distribution of participants on courses varies considerably with employment status, both within the individual country and between the countries. If we ignore students, participation in all countries is greatest for respondents who are either in work or are registered as unemployed. The lowest level of participation is amongst people over retirement age. One special condition is that a small proportion of students in Norway and Spain are not registered as participants, in spite of their studies being registered as adult education in the survey. We have no certain explanation for this. Possible explanations may be that some have misunderstood the instructions, but also that this affects newly-registered students who thus have not been active students in the last three years.

If we look at participation in the different categories of courses in relation to the respondents' employment status, we find the following picture. In all the countries, the groups who are in employment participate most on vocational and work-related courses. We find the same picture among respondents who are unemployed. Spain stands out, however, in that those who are unemployed participate just as much on general and academic courses as on vocational courses. Participation is low in all three countries amongst edults over retirement age, but this is only to be expected given the clear preference for recreational and leisure courses.

5.3 A picture of adult education: description of the most recent course

The overview of adult education in the last three years, which is shown above, shows a number of differences between the countries:

- Over a three-year period, considerably more people in the Norwegian sample had participated in adult education than was the case in Spain and Great Britain. At the same time, participation in Spain was somewhat lower than in Great Britain.

- Adult education was dominated most strongly by work-related courses in Norway whereas this was not the case in Spain.
- A clear tendency was found for those who had participated in adult education in Norway and Great Britain to have taken more courses than those who had participated in Spain. This was particularly noticeable for the vocational and work-related courses.

In order to go into the differences between the countries in greater depth, we will look more closely at the most recent course in which the participants had participated (see table 8).

5.3.1 Course providers

A number of different organisations, both public and private, provide adult education courses. We have classified course providers into six main categories: employer, school /college /university, adult education centre, trade union, private providers, and social or voluntary organisations. "Other providers" are providers who do not fall into any of these categories.

Table 8 shows the distribution of the courses into the different provider categories. Looking at all courses together, we find three major (approximately equally large) providers. The three largest providers are employers, school /college / university and private providers. There is nonetheless a difference between the countries. In Spain, employers arrange a smaller proportion of courses than in Norway in Great Britain, while private providers arrange a smaller proportion of adult education in Great Britain.

However, the picture is less distinct when one looks at general and academic courses, vocational and work-related courses and recreational and leisure courses separately. Not surprisingly, schools, colleges and universities are the main providers of more than half of the general and academic courses. The vocational and work-related courses are distributed among a number of providers, with employers being the most important provider. This is particularly true in Great Britain. Where recreational and leisure courses are concerned, the different between the countries is particularly great. In Great Britain, recreation and leisure courses are largely arranged by the education system and by adult education centres, while the majority of recreation and leisure courses in Norway and Spain are arranged by private providers and voluntary organisations.

In general, the picture of the adult education field is complex, with some major groups of providers, but also several smaller groups. Each of the main groups we have used consists of a number of different organisations and institutions. Thus the field of adult education becomes complex and difficult to describe.

Table 8 Information about the most recent course. Base = all participants in courses.

Information about the most recent course or participants	Most recent course (total)			General and academic courses			Vocational and work-related courses			Recreational and leisure courses		
	GB	Nor	Sp	GB	Nor	Sp	GB	Nor	Sp	GB	Nor	Sp
	N=651	N=1280	N=611	N=169	N=100	N=267	N=391	N=985	N=246	N=82	N=133	N=71
Organiser												
Employer	35	30	15	8	8	3	54	38	33	4	0	1
School/college/university	37	25	34	70	56	66	23	24	10	38	6	6
Adult Education Centre	10	5	5	12	13	6	3	4	3	34	8	10
Trade Union	0	5	2	0	2	0	1	6	5	0	1	1
Private providers	8	21	21	4	13	16	9	18	22	10	49	36
Social or voluntary org.	3	6	7	1	5	2	2	2	6	9	32	27
Other	7	8	16	5	3	8	8	8	22	6	5	19
Total	100	100	100	100	100	101	100	100	101	101	101	100
Duration of course												
Less than 1 week	24	42	5	2	14	1	38	46	11	1	27	0
1 - 4 weeks	8	14	12	3	1	5	12	14	20	4	19	7
1 - 3 months	14	9	22	7	9	9	12	6	35	34	28	24
4 - 6 months	8	8	12	7	13	8	6	7	15	15	13	20
7 – 12 months	17	8	24	27	15	33	13	8	11	20	4	34
1 - 2 years	13	7	11	17	18	14	12	7	7	9	1	11
More than 2 years	17	12	15	38	30	30	8	11	2	18	9	3
Total	101	100	101	101	100	100	101	99	101	101	101	99
Weekly time consume												
1 - 5 hours	33	17	20	27	18	8	26	12	25	79	52	47
6 – 10 hours	22	19	25	19	12	20	25	21	30	16	17	25
11 – 15 hours	8	10	8	10	5	7	9	11	8	2	9	9
16 – 20 hours	8	12	14	8	13	14	9	12	14	2	14	13
21 – 25 hours	6	6	9	6	5	13	7	6	6	0	2	1
26 hours or more	23	35	25	31	47	38	25	38	16	0	7	6
Total	100	99	101	101	100	100	101	100	99	99	101	101

NOTE: total varies from 99 to 101 due to rounding of decimals.

5.3.2 Duration of course

A comparison of the duration of the courses in the three countries in the study, showed that the course picture is very different in the three countries. The duration of the courses was shortest in Norway and longest in Spain. Taking all the courses together, the results show that 42 % of the courses in Norway were less than one week in duration, while only 24 % of the courses in Great Britain and 5 % and Spain were as short as this. Looking at somewhat longer courses, courses which last more than six months, it can be seen that this applies to 28 % of the courses in Norway, 46 % of courses in Great Britain and 49 % of courses in Spain. This is connected with the fact that work-related courses have a more dominant place in Norway than in the other countries, where general and academic courses comprise a greater part of adult education.

Table 8 shows the duration of the different types of course. The tendency for courses to be shorter in Norway than in the other countries applies to all types of courses. The difference between Great Britain and Spain primarily concerned the duration of vocational and work-related courses. This can probably be explained by the fact that a greater proportion of the vocational and work-related courses in Great Britain were courses arranged by employers.

These are, to a large extent, short courses which are not intended to provide formal qualifications.

5.3.3 Weekly time consumption

Norway stood out from the other two countries in that those who took part in adult education used more time per week in learning. This broadens the picture of adult education in Norway, and to some extent in Great Britain, as dominated by short, but rather intensive courses.

5.3.4 Participation during work hours and paid leave

Table 9 shows the proportion of those participants who were employed who participated during work hours in the three countries. It is important here to note that the percentages are calculated from the participants who where in employment at the time they took the course. For both general and academic courses, and for vocational courses, the results show that it is much more common to participate during working hours in Great Britain and Norway than it is in Spain. This is particularly true of vocational courses and table 9 shows that around two out of three participants who were in employment had taken their most recent course during working hours in Great Britain and Norway.

These results can explain the low participation in vocational courses in Spain. The long working day in Spain, which is due to a longer break in the middle of the day, combined with fewer opportunities to take courses during working hours, must be part of the reason for the low participation on vocational courses in Spain.

Table 9 Proportion of employed participants who have participated in courses during work hours.

	Great Britain		Norway		Spain	
Type of course	Base	%	Base	%	Base	%
General and academic course	113	39	51	33	82	12
Vocational course	338	68	855	71	189	41
Recreational/leisure course	32	16	84	4	18	**

** N < 20

5.4 Self-confidence and perceived value of learning

Research into motivation has shown that cognitive and emotional processes are significant both for people's choice of activities in which to participate and the amount of input and perseverance they demonstrate. For a general overview, see chapter three. In this section, we will look at the significance of three general psychological variables for participation in adult education: self-confidence, intrinsic interest value of learning and extrinsic utility value of learning.

All the respondents, both those who had participated and those who had not participated in adult education, were asked to respond to statements about themselves. These were general statements which were not related to any given course; nor did the statements make any reference as to whether the respondents had participated or not participated in adult education. The respondents replied to each statement using a five-point scale from "agree" to "disagree".

The statements formed the basis for a statistical analysis which is described as factor analysis. This is a technique which, in this case, is based on the assumption that underlying several statements we may find more general self-perception and motivation factors. The purpose of the factor analyses was to analyse whether the anticipated factors (self-worth, self-confidence in learning, intrinsic interest value of learning, and extrinsic utility value of learning) could be identified, whether they diverge clearly from each other and whether there was a statistical basis for summing up the answers to the statements which belong the same category on a total scale, which could be used in later analyses. The factor analyses were based on all the respondents in the three samples. Separate analyses based on the samples in each country confirmed the result of the analysis.

Eight of the statements formed three identifiable factors: self-confidence, intrinsic interest value of learning and extrinsic utility value of learning. The result of the factor analysis is shown in appendix 2, whereas table 10 shows the concrete statements which form each of the factors. The *self-confidence* factor consisted of evaluations of the extent to which respondents accepted themselves, valued themselves and had confidence in their own ability to learn. Thus, statements designed to measure general self-worth and self-confidence in learning could not be separated into two different factors, and we decided to term the one factor "self-confidence". The *intrinsic interest value of learning* factor consisted of respondents' general desire to learn and their perception that learning is fun, while the *extrinsic utility value of learning* factor was connected with expectations of outcome or utility value. The reliability of the measurements for each factor was tested using Cronbach's alpha. These values were relatively low for the *self-confidence* and *intrinsic value* factors, while the value was very satisfactory for the *extrinsic value* factor. Based on the result of the factor analysis, the factors were nonetheless used in further analyses.

Table 10 Psychological factors and items defining each factor.

Factors	Statements
Factor 1: Self confidence (alpha = .56)	I am a valuable person, at least as valuable as others I am satisfied with myself If there is something I want to learn, I know that I can do it
Factor 2: Intrinsic interest value of learning (alpha = .67)	Learning something new is fun I have always wanted to learn more If I were to participate in education or training it would be because I think learning in itself is fun
Factor 3: Extrinsic utility value of learning (alpha = .83)	I have nothing to gain by further education and training For myself I see no purpose in further education and training

In the further analyses, the statements which comprised each of the factors was summarised. The intercorrelations between these total scores were small and varied between .09 and .32. The three psychological variables could therefore be considered and analysed as separate and relatively independent variables.

Thereafter the respondents in all three countries were put into one large group, which was then re-divided into three groups of approximately the same size with high, medium or low scores for each of the factors of self-confidence, intrinsic interest value and extrinsic utility value. Thus, the split points between high, medium, and low scores were the same in each country. Table 11 reveals that, relatively speaking, the Spanish respondents had lower scores on both intrinsic interest value and extrinsic utility value of learning than the British and the Norwegian respondents, whereas the Norwegian respondents had somewhat higher scores on self-confidence than the British and Spanish respondents.

Table 11 Percentage of respondents with high, medium and low self-confidence, intrinsic interest value of learning and extrinsic utility value of learning. Base = all respondents.

Categories	Self confidence			Intrinsic interest value of learning			Extrinsic utility value of learning		
	GB	Nor	Sp	GB	Nor	Sp	GB	Nor	Sp
	N = 1552	N = 1825	N = 1899	N = 1549	N = 1827	N = 1905	N = 1553	N = 1828	N = 1914
High	28	37	28	27	24	22	49	43	31
Medium	38	42	30	48	55	37	26	33	42
Low	35	21	42	25	21	41	25	24	27
Total	101	100	100	100	100	100	100	100	100

NOTE: total varies from 100 to 101 due to rounding of decimals

Table 12 shows the proportion who have participated in adult education in the last three years for respondents with high, average and low self-confidence, intrinsic interest value and extrinsic utility value, respectively. Self-confidence was not systematically related to participation in adult education in Great Britain and was weakly related to participation in Norway. However, there was a strong relation between participation and self-confidence in Spain, where 42 % of respondents with high self-confidence had participated compared to 25 % of respondents with low self-confidence.

Table 12 Percentage participation in courses during the last 3 years within groups with high, medium and low self-confidence, intrinsic interest value of learning and extrinsic utility value of learning.

	Self confidence			Intrinsic interest value of learning			Extrinsic utility value of learning		
	GB	Nor	Sp	GB	Nor	Sp	GB	Nor	Sp
High	39	74	42	51	69	45	63	85	55
Medium	43	71	34	43	73	38	33	72	26
Low	42	61	25	28	63	21	10	40	17

** N < 20

Intrinsic interest value of learning was strongly related to participation in both Great Britain and Spain, where the participation rate increased strongly and systematically with increased intrinsic value of learning. In the Norwegian sample, however, intrinsic value of learning was only weakly and not systematically related to participation.

Extrinsic utility value of learning was strongly related to participation in all three countries. In Great Britain, where extrinsic value of learning had the greatest impact on participation, the participation rate for respondents with high scores on extrinsic value was six times the rate of respondents with low scores on extrinsic value. However, the impact of extrinsic value was very strong in all countries.

In summary, the self-perception and motivation variables had a somewhat different impact on participation in the three countries. A common feature was that extrinsic utility value of learning was the variable which influenced participation in all countries most strongly, but the impact was stronger in Great Britain and Spain than in Norway. Also intrinsic interest value of learning had a strong impact on participation in Great Britain and Spain, but not in Norway, whereas the impact of self-confidence was strong only in Spain. It is important to note that these tendencies were found irrespective of gender, age, and level of education (see appendix 3). However, in all countries the impact of intrinsic interest value of learning was particularly strong for respondents between 60 and 79 years of age.

Based on the results, we can safely conclude that psychological variables, particularly the perceived extrinsic utility value of learning, are very important determinants for participation in adult education. We can only speculate about the difference between the countries. One possible interpretation may be based on the level of education in the three countries. We find the lowest level of education in the Spanish sample, where 70 % of the respondents either lack formal education or only have primary school education. Thus, a large majority of the Spanish sample lacks educational experiences after leaving primary school. This may explain why low self-confidence has such a large effect on participation in education.

The impact of the psychological variables was somewhat smaller in the Norwegian sample than in the British and the Spanish sample. Possible explanations may be that the scale of participation is very high in Norway, that the level of education is high and that a large majority of the courses are work-related and take place during working hours. Both the high level of education and the high rate of participation may result in a strong belief that continuing education is important, which may overshadow the impact of both self-confidence and intrinsic interest value of learning. Additionally, the high percentage of adult education which is work-related may indicate a strong stimulation, or possible pressure, at the work place to participate in education.

6 MOTIVATION FOR PARTICIPATION

6.1 Reasons for participation

In order to chart the motives of participants for participating in adult education, those who had participated in the course the last three years were given 14 potential motives for participating in such education. Each of the 14 reasons is shown in table 13. The respondents in all three countries were asked to evaluate which was the most important and the next most important for them. In addition the Norwegian respondents were asked to evaluate the significance of each of these 14 possible motives for their participation on their most recent course. These evaluations were made using a four-point scale, where 1 stood for "very important" and 4 represented "not important". Both these evaluations will be used in the analyses in this chapter.

6.1.1 The most important reasons for participating on courses

Table 13 shows the percentage of participants in Great Britain, Norway and Spain who indicated each of the 14 motives as the main motive and second most important motive for participation.

Table 13 Most important and second most important reason for participating in the most recent course. Base = all participants in courses during the last 3 years.

Reason for participating in courses	Main reason			Second most important reason		
	GB N= 651	Nor N= 1280	Sp N= 618	GB N= 651	Nor N= 1280	SP N= 618
to get a (recognised) qualification	14	34	24	14	21	21
to perform my work better	26	16	8	12	22	11
I am interested in the subject or topic	15	14	7	12	14	12
to get a job	9	10	34	5	5	8
to develop myself as a person	6	5	11	15	10	20
I had no choice – my employer decided	10	8	2	4	3	1
to change the type of work I do	5	3	1	5	4	2
to help me get on a future course	1	3	3	4	4	3
to meet (new) people	0	1	0	4	5	3
I enjoy reading and learning	1	1	1	6	4	2
to get a job with another employer	2	1	1	2	3	1
to improve my self-confidence	1	1	1	5	2	3
to be promoted	5	1	4	6	1	8
to have something to do	1	1	2	2	1	3
other reasons	3	4	2	2	3	2
don't know/no answer	1	0	0	2	0	0
Total	100	103	101	100	102	100

NOTE: total varies from 100 to 103 due to rounding of decimals

Six reasons stood out because more than 10 % of the respondents in at least one country regarded it as the main reason for participating. These reasons were: *to get a (recognised) qualification, to perform my work better, I am interested in the subject or topic, to get a job, to develop myself as a person, and I had no choice - my employer decided.* Four of these reasons are job-related (see below).

There were still some major differences between the countries. The work-related reasons differed greatly. The most important work-related reason in Great Britain was "to perform my work better", whereas the most important work-related reason in Spain was "to get a job". The most important reason for participating at all in Norway, was "to get a (recognised) qualification". Factor analysis revealed that this reason also was perceived as a work-related reason (see table 14). Thus, work-related reasons were important motives for participation in all countries, but they differed with respect to the goals of the participants.

6.1.2 Categories of reasons

In order further to analyse reasons for participating, we conducted a factor analysis of the Norwegian data. As pointed out in chapter 5, factor analysis is a statistical analysis that is used to find general factors underlying several concrete statements. In this case we looked for general motivation factors underlying the concrete reasons for participating. One problem is that this could only be done for the Norwegian data, because the Norwegian respondents were asked to judge each reason on a four-point scale. We therefore factor analysed the reasons for participating given by the Norwegian respondents. Then, assuming that the factors (categories) found could be generalised to all three samples, we analysed motivational categories in all samples. This assumption was strengthened by factor analyses of judgement of benefit of adult education, which in all countries revealed the same factor pattern as we found for reasons for participating (see chapter 7).

The first step in these analyses was to factor analyse the reasons given by the Norwegian respondents. The factor analysis revealed that 10 of the reasons formed three identifiable factors (groups of reasons): *personal development, new work situation, and carrying out one's work better*. The reasons included in each factor and Cronbach's alpha for the factors are shown in table 14, whereas the factor loadings are shown in appendix 4. The three motivation factors were weakly correlated (correlations between 0.21 and 0.34). Thus, the motivational factors turn out to be relatively independent, which also means that work-related motives neither predict nor prevent motives related to personal development.

Table 14 Reasons for participation (factor analysis, Norway).

Factors:		Statements
Factor 1: (alpha = .73)	Personal development	to develop myself as a person to improve my self confidence I enjoy reading and learning I am interested in the subject/topic
Factor 2: (alpha = .65)	New work situation	to get a job with another employer to get a job to change the type of work I do to be promoted
Factor 3: (alpha = .60)	Carrying out one's work better	to perform my work better to get a (recognised) qualification

Factor 1, personal development, comprised the following reasons: "develop myself as a person", "improve my self confidence", enjoy reading and learning", and "interested in the subject/topic". Both factor 2 and 3 consisted of work-related reasons. Factor 2, *new work situation*, consisted of four concrete reasons: "get a job", "get a job with another employer", "change type of work", and "be promoted". Factor 3, *carrying out one's work better*, consisted of only two reasons: "perform my work better" and "get a (recognised) qualification".

Thus, the results show that the reason "to get a (recognised) qualification" was perceived as a work-related reason by the respondents. The analysis also confirmed that there was a clear distinction between two work-related motives, to change one's work situation and to be better able to carry out one's work. The factor pattern was very clear, with high loadings on the relevant factor and no loadings above 0.4 on any other factor.

6.1.3 The importance of each category

The next step in the analyses was to create new observed variables or categories based on the three motivation categories. A respondent answering one of the four reasons indicating factor 1 (personal development) as the most important reason for participating, was identified as a respondent for whom personal development was the most important motivation. Similarly, other respondents were identified as having either "new work situation" or "carrying out their work better" as their main motivation. This procedure was carried out for all respondents, not only respondents in the Norwegian sample. Consequently, we could analyse the percentage of respondents in each country who had *personal development, new work situation,* and *carrying out one's work better* as their main reason for participating.

The results are shown in table 15. Four of the concrete reasons put to the respondents did not fit into the factor pattern. In table 15 these reasons are joined together and called "other reasons". That does not mean that they constitute a homogeneous category, but is done to illustrate the proportion of the sample who had main reasons for participating other one of the three categories from the factor analysis. In table 15 we have also shown, as a separate reason those respondents who stated that they had not had any choice.

Table 15 Distribution of categories of main reasons for participating. Base = all participants in courses.

Categories of reasons	GB N = 646	Nor N = 1279	Sp N = 618
Factor 1. Personal development	24	20	20
Factor 2. New work situation	22	15	40
Factor 3. Carrying out one's work better	40	49	32
Had no choice	10	8	2
Other reasons	5	8	7
Total	**101**	**100**	**101**

NOTE: total varies from 100 to 101 due to rounding of decimals

Table 15 shows that work-related motives are the most important motives for the majority of participants. Seen together, work-related motives were the most important motivation for participating for 62 %, 64 %, and 72 % of the respondents from Great Britain, Norway, and Spain, respectively. However, as pointed out above, for participants in Great Britain and Norway the most important work-related motive was to improve one's skills in order to perform one's work better. In contrast, for participants in Spain the most important work-related motive was to get a (new) job or to change one's work situation.

Even though work-related motives dominated, personal development was the main reason for participating for 20-24 % of the respondents in all countries. Moreover, it was the second most important motive for another 40-45 % of the respondents in all countries. Thus, personal development is an important additional motive for a majority of respondents who have work-related main reasons for participating. This is a very important result, because it indicates that the change in adult education towards more work-related learning may not have reduced participants' desire for the learning to result in personal development. This conclusion should be noted by providers and organisers of adult education. (see also chapter 7 on benefit of participation).

The motivation for participating in adult education may vary somewhat for different groups of participants, and we will therefore look at what has been the most import motive for participation for some groups of participants (see also appendix 5). In all three countries, women put more emphasis than men on self-development as a reason for participation. Men put more emphasis than women on increasing their competence in order to be better equipped to carry out their work. It seems therefore that pragmatic motives are more important for men in the three countries, while women are more concerned with self-development. An interesting interpretation, that needs further investigation, is that women are more concerned with self-development because they are given less challenging work and less oportunity for promotion at the workplace.

The difference between the age groups is marked in all three countries. Personal development increases with age and is the most important motivation for participating for respondents over 60 years of age in all countries. We have previously pointed out that the work-related motivation in Spain differed from the work-related motivation in Great Britain, in that the goal of the Spanish participants was, to a larger extent, to change their working situation. However, this difference between the countries only applied for the two youngest age groups. From the age of 45, once one is more established in the labour market, the main work-related motivation was to be able to perform one's work better for Spanish participants as well.

The reasons for participating did not differ greatly for respondents with different level of education. Still, there was a clear tendency that respondents with a high level of education were more motivated to learn to perform their work better. As could be expected, learning to perform one's work better was a stronger motivation for participants on work-related courses whereas personal development was the main motivation for participants on recreational and leisure courses.

6.2 Intention to participate in future learning

All respondents were asked about their interests and wishes connected with participation in adult education in the future. There are differences between expressing a wish or estimating the probability of participation and actual participation. Actual participation is not only dependent on wishes and motives, but also on the extent of any barriers. The questions which will be analysed here are therefore hypothetical, and must be interpreted as indications of motivation and attitude. In order to make the evaluations as concrete as possible, the questions were related to the coming three years.

6.2.1 Likelihood of starting a course in the next three years

One question which was put to all the respondents concerned the likelihood of doing a new course during the next three years. The possible answers were " very likely" "fairly likely" "fairly unlikely" and "very unlikely". In the whole sample, 39 % in Great Britain, 64% in

Norway and 34 % in Spain replied that it was very likely or fairly likely that they would take part in new courses (table 16). These suggestions lie close to the actual participation over the previous three years and therefore demonstrate great realism in the responces. The small deviations in relation to participation in the three previous years, however, go in different directions. In Great Britain and Norway the anticipated participation in the next three years is somewhat below the registered participation for the last three years, while in Spain there are rather more who say they will participate in courses in the future, compared with the actual number of participants in the past three years. Since the differences between previous participation and anticipated participation in the future is small, these differences should be interpreted with caution. A possible conclusion may be that the opportunities for participation are weaker in Spain than in the other two countries, partly due to the organisation of the working day and also because fewer courses are offered at the workplace, and that the wish to participate in Spain therefore is greater than the actual participation.

Table 16 Percentage who consider it as "very likely " or "likely" that they will take courses the next 3 years. Base = all respondents.

	Total		
	Great Britain	Norway	Spain
Type of course	N = 1550	N = 1828	N = 1916
All types of courses	39	64	34
General and academic course	23	11	16
Vocational course	29	54	24
Recreational and leisure course	17	34	15

The respondents were also asked to evaluate the probability of participating in different types of courses (see table 16). In this connection, the courses are classified in the same way as previously, into general and academic courses, vocational and work-related courses and recreational and leisure courses.

In Norway and Spain, the probability of participation on general and academic courses corresponded closely with the actual participation on corresponding courses in the previous three years (see table 4), while the anticipated participation on such courses in Great Britain is much higher than the actual participation on such courses. A possible reason for this is that Great Britain has a much larger proportion of respondents without formal education qualifications. The result indicates that many of these would like to complete a formal education. Making this possible appears to be an important task in Great Britain.

The evaluation of the probability for participation on vocational and work-related courses in the next three years deviates little from the actual participation in Great Britain and Norway. In Spain, however, the probability of participation on such courses was evaluated as being much higher than the actual participation. This indicates that the low participation on vocational and work-related courses in Spain, compared to the Great Britain and Norway, is due to lack of opportunities and courses rather than a lack of desire or motivation for participation.

The probability of participating on recreational and leisure courses in the next three years is evaluated in all three countries as high when compared with the real participation in the three previous years. These results can be interpreted as the interest in participation on recreation and leisure courses being much greater than what, in practice, proves to be feasible. In all probability, this is due to the fact that recreation and leisure courses are taken in people's leisure time, and that practical problems can get in the way more easily for participation in leisure time than for participation during working hours. However, it may also indicate that when it is necessary to prioritise, courses which are relevant to working conditions are given higher priority than courses which are connected with leisure time interests.

One interesting question is the extent to which adults who have participated on courses in the last three years think it likely that they will participate in coming years. Table 17 shows that the majority who had participated in the last three years in the three countries covered by the study also consider it possible that they will participate in the next three years (respectively 64 %, 79 % and 71 % in Great Britain, Norway and Spain). By way of comparison, respectively only 21 %, 30 % and 16 % of those who had not participated in the last three years regarded participation as probable in the next period. This can be interpreted in different ways. One possible interpretation is that those who have participated feel that the rewards have been great, and that they therefore wish to participate in the future. Such an interpretation corresponds well with the participants' evaluations of the benefits of the courses (see chapter 7). An alternative, but not conflicting interpretation, can be based on the fact that the great majority of participants had taken part in courses which are related to their work and which to a large extent take place during working hours. The result can then be interpreted to show that those who had such opportunities previously are in positions in their working life when they feel that similar opportunities will be available in the future. There is every reason to look at this interpretation more closely in research projects which are designed for this purpose, since it also implies that a number of employees have few opportunities for education and increasing their competence in connection with their work (see also chapter 6.2.3, table 19).

Table 17 Percentage of respondents who consider it "likely" or "very likely" that they will do courses the next 3 years, by participation in courses the last 3-years. Base = all respondents.

	GB	Nor	Sp
Participation in courses last 3 years	N = 1550	N = 1828	N = 1916
Respondents who has participated in courses during the last 3 years	64	79	71
Respondents who has not participated in courses during the last 3 years	21	30	16

6.2.2 Variables predicting likelihood of starting a course in the next three years

Path analyses were conducted in order to explore variables predicting the respondents' perceived likelihood of participating during the next three years. As predictor variables we chose to use gender, age, level of education, self-confidence, intrinsic interest value of learning and extrinsic utility value of learning.

One path analysis was conducted including respondents from all three countries (figure 1). Separate path analyses, based on respondents from each country, were also conducted in order to explore possible differences between the countries in the impact of the predictor variables (see appendix 6).

Figure 1 reveal that 32 % of the variance in perceived likelihood of participating during the next three years was explained by the predictor variables. Both intrinsic learning value and extrinsic utility value factors predicted likelihood of participating whereas self-confidence did not. Age and level of education influenced likelihood of participating both directly and indirectly through intrinsic and extrinsic value of learning. In other words, both age and level of education partly affected likelihood of participating irrespective of perceived value of learning, but also affected perceived value of learning which in turn affected likelihood of participating.

It is important to notice that gender had no effect on self-confidence, value of learning or likelihood of participating. We should also point out that with increasing age the extrinsic utility value of learning decreased strongly, whereas age had no effect on intrinsic interest value of learning. This means, for instance, that elderly people may have an intrinsic motivation to learn that does not manifest itself in actual participation in adult education. A very important task is to examine further the reasons for this, in order to offer opportunities that are well adapted to their needs and interests.

Appendix 6 show the results of path analyses conducted separately for each sample. The main picture of these analyses is that, by and large, they present the same pattern of results.

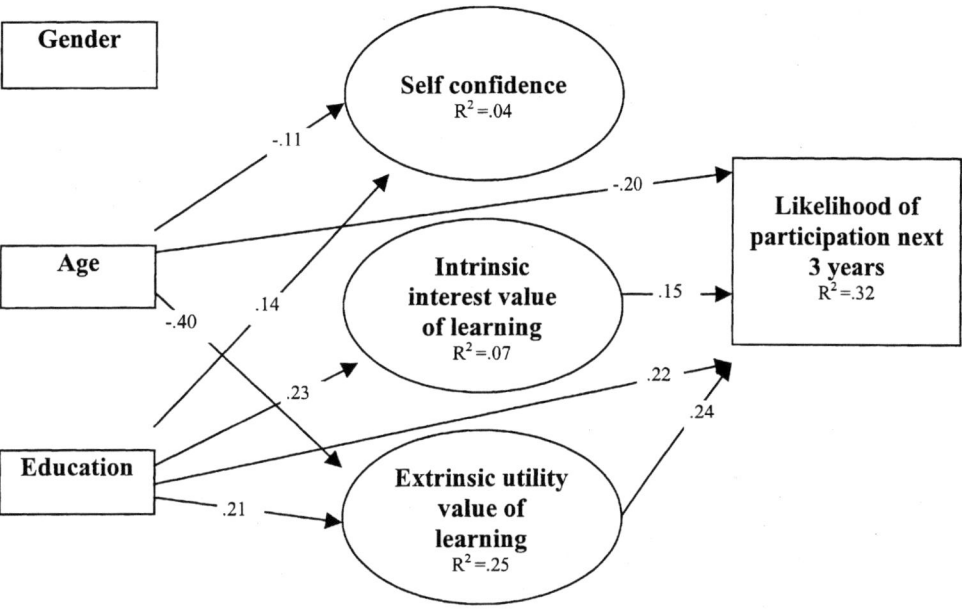

Note: Beta values below .10 are not included in the figure.

Figure 1 Path analysis with probable participation in the next three years as the dependent variable.

6.2.3 Opportunities and desire for courses in working hours

The respondents who were in employment were asked to evaluate the opportunity for participating in education during normal working hours. There were great differences in how the respondents who where in employment in the three countries evaluated the chances of taking time off from work to participate in courses. While 50 % in Great Britain and 67 % in Norway considered that they had such opportunities, only 28 % of Spanish employees confirmed that they could take time off from work to take part in courses or education (table 18).

The probability for taking leave, with or without pay, was evaluated differently in the three countries. While 63 % of respondents who were in employment in Norway and 49 % in Great Britain evaluated it as very likely or fairly likely that they would obtain paid leave of absence in order take a course during working hours, the corresponding group in Spain comprised only 24 % of the respondents. Corresponding results were found for leave without pay.

These results can probably explain much of the difference between the countries regarding participation in work-related or vocational courses over the last three years. These results showed that participation had been greatest in Norway and lowest in Spain. The respondents' evaluation of the chances of having time off work, or both paid and unpaid leave from work, in order to follow courses, follow the same pattern of differences between the countries. This indicates that the differences between the countries may, to a large extent, be due to differences in employers' attitudes to, and evaluation of, further education amongst their employees.

Table 18 Percentage of employed respondents who are able to get time off from work to follow courses and percentage who consider it likely they would get paid or unpaid leave. Base = all employed.

	Total		
	Great Britain N = 811	**Norway** N = 1266	**Spain** N = 815
Able to get time off from work	57	67	28
Likelihood getting paid leave	49	63	24
Likelihood getting unpaid leave	40	63	24

The results for Great Britain and Norway confirm the impression obtained by analysing participation in the last three years, namely that employers either initiate or create opportunities for extensive course participation. Many employees in these countries, in Norway in particular, therefore have great opportunities to increase their competence connected with their work. At the same time, there is a large group which does not have, or does not believe it has, such opportunities. Analyses of the participation is over the last three years show that this particularly affects employees with low levels of education.

We also studied whether there were differences in the opportunities which respondents in employment felt they had for going on courses during working hours and for obtaining leave when we divided them into sub-groups according to gender, age and education (appendix 7). We found no significant differences between men and women in any of the countries. We also found the same tendencies as we have shown in table 18 for the different age groups. However, the result showed clear differences between respondents with different levels of education. In all three countries, respondents with college or university-level education had greater expectations of obtaining leave in order to participate in courses and greater expectations of obtaining paid and unpaid leave during the education period, than the groups with lower levels of education. The differences are relatively great in all three countries and can probably explain some of the difference in participation for respondents with different levels of education.

We also analysed whether there was any relation between participation in adult education over the last three years and the respondents' evaluation of the possibility of getting time off work and getting paid or unpaid leave (table 19). The result shows that those who had participated in adult education in the last three years evaluated their chances of participating during working hours much higher than those whose had not participated in the last three years. The difference is particularly great in Spain, but is also significant in Great Britain. The result indicates that the chance of participating during working hours is a key factor for participation in work-related adult education. However this opportunity varies considerably between the countries in this study. An evaluation should therefore be made of the possibility of further education being regulated more stringently through the introduction of rights and through financial measures. In Norway, the "competence reform " is one element in such work.

Table 19 Percentage of employed respondents (total and by participation during the last 3 years) who are able to get time off from work to follow courses and percentage who consider it likely that they will obtain paid or unpaid leave. Base = all employed.

	Total			Participated in courses during the last 3 years					
				Yes			No		
	GB	Nor	Sp	GB	Nor	Sp	GB	Nor	Sp
	N= 811	N= 1266	N= 815	N= 446	N= 1016	N= 306	N= 366	N= 256	N= 517
Able to get time off from work	57	67	28	69	69	50	42	56	15
Likelihood getting paid leave	49	63	24	61	67	39	34	47	15
Likelihood getting unpaid leave	40	63	24	45	65	37	33	57	16

7 BENEFITS OF ADULT EDUCATION

Questions on reasons for participating and the benefits of participation were both connected with the participants' most recent course. Some of the respondents were participating on their most recent course when the interview took place. Questions on benefits were not put to this group. However the majority of respondents were not participating on courses at the time of the interview, but referred to a completed course when they were interviewed. This group were questioned on the benefits they had obtained from their most recent course.

7.1 Categories of benefit

As with reasons for participation (see chapter 6), the respondents were also asked to respond to a number of statements, with a total of 13 statements.. These 13 statements were identical in content to 13 of the statements of reasons for participation, but were now to be answered taking into account the benefits of the course. For each statement, the respondents should reply whether they obtained great benefit, relatively large benefit, relatively little benefit or no benefit when they looked at the statement in relation to the benefit of the most recent course in which they had participated.

Questions on benefit were put to the participants in all three countries. Responses to the 13 statements about the benefit of the most recent course were factor analysed. When analysing responses from all participants in all countries, we found three benefit factors identical to the motivation factors shown in table 14; *personal development, new work situation,* and *carrying out one's work better* (appendix 8). Three statements did not fit into this factor structure: "to help get on a future course", "to meet new people", and "to have something to do".

We then conducted separate analyses for participants in each country. The Norwegian and the Spanish responses revealed the same factor structure as described above. However, the analyses of the British data revealed a two-factor solution, not discriminating between different work-related goals. Running an analysis of the British data asking for three factors showed that "getting a (recognised) qualification" was associated with changing one's work situation in Great Britain, whereas is was associated with performing one's work better in Spain and Norway. This is probably due to differences in the statements in the three countries. The statement in Great Britain emphasised "a recognised qualification" whereas the term recognised was not included in the Norwegian and Spanish questionnaire. Particularly in Norway there is an awareness of a distinction between formal and informal qualification, the formal (or recognised) qualification being most important when applying for a job.

The tables below are organised according to the result of the factor analyses, presenting different benefits under four headings: *personal development, new work situation, carrying out one's work better,* and *other benefits.*

7.2 Judgement of benefit in the three countries

Table 20 shows how each possible aspect of benefit was judged in each country. For the purpose of analysing what kinds of benefit were evaluated most positively, we looked at the proportion of participants judging the most recent course as being either "very useful" or "useful". We then focused on benefits judged as "very useful" or "useful" by at least 60 % of the participants. Such a procedure shows major differences between the countries. In Norway only three types of benefit were judged as "very useful" or "useful" by more than 60 % of the participants. In comparison, four types of benefit were judged as "very useful" or "useful" by more than 60 % of the participants in Great Britain, whereas nine types of benefit were judged equally positively by more than 60 % of the participants in Spain.

Care should be taken not to draw too hasty conclusions from these results. Nevertheless, the results are quite thought provoking. They mean that in Norway, where the scale of participation was the highest, the perceived benefit of the courses was the lowest, or was narrowed down to a few aspects of benefit. By comparison, in Spain, where the scale of participation was the lowest, the perceived benefit was the highest, with a broad range of perceived benefits.

Norway is approaching a situation where most adults, at least at some point, are involved in some kind of formal learning - particularly at the workplace. Seen from a participant's perspective, this may mean that participation in adult education has become so commonplace that participation does not always build on any strong motivation or is followed by any great input. In the worst case, learning at work may simply have become a welcome change from work itself. In Spain, we have seen that participation in adult education is much lower. This is particularly true for learning at the workplace. This may mean that interest in participation is much greater than the opportunities for participation, and motivation and input among those who participate is therefore greater. This reasoning builds on the assumption that there is a connection between the benefit of participants and their motivation and input connected with learning.

Table 20 Usefulness of most recent course. Percentage of participants who responded "very useful "or "useful" to the given statements. Base = all participants who had completed a course during the last 3 years.

The course was useful	Great Britain N = 304	Norway N = 967	Spain N = 340
Personal development:			
to develop myself as a person	80	44	91
to improve my self-confidence	76	38	81
I really enjoyed reading and learning	54	41	71
my interest in the subject or topic was stimulated	81	79	86
New work situation:			
to get a job with another employer	38	16	24
to get a job	48	22	45
to change the type of work I do	38	24	29
to be promoted	35	9	48
Carrying out one's work better:			
to get a (recognised) qualification	53	76	83
to perform my work better	74	68	73
Other:			
to help me get on a future course	50	35	63
to meet (new) people	59	34	72
to have something to do	56	11	68

However, the result can also be interpreted from a provider perspective. With the expansion of adult education in Norway, the demand has become great. Many courses are planned and arranged, and great financial interest is connected with the implementation of courses. The question arises whether the tempo has become too fast to ensure sufficient attention to quality assurance. Where participation is lower, for example in Spain, quality assurance of the courses can thus be given greater attention.

These discussions focus on two main interpretations of the benefits experienced as being lowest where participation is greatest; one interpretation which explains the results from the participants' motivation and involvement, and another interpretation which explains the result from the quality assurance of planning and implementation of the courses. Both interpretations, however, are speculations which cannot be defended on the basis of the data at hand. On the contrary, these results and the provisional interpretations should be used as the basis for more in-depth analysis in later research. A related question is whether the frequency of participation in adult education can reach an optimal level, and whether participation beyond this level for different reasons can reduce the value of learning if specific measures for quality assurance are not implemented.

Up until now, however, we have only looked at how many forms of benefit participants feel they have had. Just as interesting is the question about the areas where participants have had the greatest benefit from adult education. Two areas distinguish themselves in that the benefit was great for the participants in all three countries. These concern (a) stimulating interest in the subject which was followed up after the course and (b) the participants feeling they were prepared to carry out their work better. In Norway and Spain, many participants also felt they had developed better qualifications. (Here, the British results were not entirely comparable, since they were asked about *formal* qualifications).

Two other areas stand out in that the benefit was great in Great Britain and Spain, while it was not evaluated as being so great in Norway. These concern (a) personal development and (b) improved self-confidence. This result gives further reasons to analyse the content and quality of adult education in Norway. It is also interesting to note that personal development and development of self-confidence were not particularly great motives for participating in adult education in any of the countries. It is all the more positive that the benefit was evaluated so positively in these areas.

7.3 Benefits for different groups of participants

Appendix 9 shows how different groups of respondents in each country evaluated the benefit of the most recent course they attended. The main tendency can be read from appendix 9, which is that the same pattern runs throughout, independent of gender, age or level of education. The benefit of adult education, as evaluated by the participants themselves, seems to be relatively independent of these variables. Independent of gender, age and level of education, the participants evaluate the benefit relatively similarly. This is true for both the evaluation of how great the benefit was and in what way the benefit has been greatest. This means on the whole that the groups who participate little in adult education, the elderly and adults with low levels of education, have the same feeling of benefit as other participants when they first take part.

Nonetheless some differences between the groups can be pointed out. All four evaluations which belong to the personal development category were evaluated more positively by women than men in the Norwegian sample. Corresponding results were not found for participants in Great Britain and Spain. With increasing age, the participants in all countries evaluated the benefit in the form of changes in the work situation as lower. However, there was no great difference between the age groups under 60 where benefit in the form of being able to carry out one's work better was concerned. The results concerning benefit therefore provide good arguments for working to even out the difference between the age groups with regard to participation.

For some forms of benefit, we found differences between participants with high and low levels of education. In Norway, benefit in the form of increased self-confidence and getting a job was greater for those who had low levels of education than for those who had high levels of education. In Great Britain, benefit in the form of being promoted was greatest for participants with high levels of education, while participants with low levels of education has, to a large extent, been given new tasks at work. Benefits in the form of having learnt to carry out one's work better are evaluated in all countries as somewhat greater for those who had the highest levels of education.

An interesting result was that the benefit in the form of personal development varied little with the type of course in which the participants had taken part. On the other hand, as expected, the work-related benefit was lower for participants on recreational and leisure courses than other participants.

8 BARRIERS TO PARTICIPATION

The present study shows that many more adults participate in organised learning in Norway than in Great Britain and Spain. We have also shown that in the three-year period covered by the study, 30 % of the sample in Norway had not participated in any form of organised learning, while the corresponding figures for Great Britain and Spain were respectively 59 % and 68 %. However, participation was very unevenly distributed between the different groups of each population (see chapter 5). The majority of those who have not participated are to be found amongst the oldest and those with the lowest levels of education.

It cannot be a goal in itself for the whole population to participate in organised learning at any time. On the other hand it must be a goal to create the best possible opportunities for participation. We therefore need a clearer picture of the reasons for not participating in adult education. In this chapter, we will analyse barriers and obstacles to participation.

8.1 Reasons for not participating in courses

In previous studies of barriers to participation, a distinction has been made between external and internal (psychological) barriers (see chapter 3). In this study, the respondents were presented with 19 potential barriers. These were drawn up to cover as many barriers as possible, both internal and external. Each of the 19 barriers is shown in table 21. The respondents who had not participated in adult education in the three-year period in each of the three countries, evaluated which of the 19 possible barriers had been the most important and the next most important reason for their non-participation. In Norway, the non-participants were also asked to evaluate the significance each of the 19 possible barriers. This was done on the four point scale, where 1 meant "great significance" and 4 meant "no significance". Both these evaluations will be used in analyses in this chapter.

Table 21 shows the percentage of those who had not participated in adult education in Great Britain, Norway and Spain who pointed out each of the 19 barriers as the main reason and the next most important reason for non-participation. The table further shows the percentage who chose each of the 19 reasons either as a main reason or the next most important reason.

The table shows that five of the barriers stood out in that more than 10 % of those who had not participated in one or more of the three countries indicated each of them as important reasons. These reasons were *did not have time, not interested, felt no need to learn more, health reasons/feeling too old*, and *there was no suitable course*. In total, these barriers comprised the main reasons for 75 % of respondents who had not participated in Great Britain, 68 % in Norway and 72 % in Spain. In each of the three countries, a further 9 % replied that care obligations were the most important reasons for non-participation. If we look at the most important and second most important reasons for non-participation in adult education together, we get more or less the same picture of the barriers which are the most important as when we look at the most important reasons alone (see table 21).

Despite the fact that we have indicated five barriers which stand out as the clearly most important barriers, the results also showed great differences between the countries. Lack of time was a much more important barrier in Spain than in the other countries, but was also more important in Great Britain then in Norway. This is assumed to be connected with differences in working hours and in the way work is organised. In addition we have seen that the respondents in Spain evaluate their chances of participating in adult education during working hours as less probable than the respondents in the other countries (see chapter 6).

We also found significant differences between the countries concerning interest in education and recognised needs for more education. The psychological barriers were greatest in Great Britain and least in Spain.

Table 21 Main reason and second most important reason for not participating in courses during the last 3 years. Base = all non-participants.

Reason for not doing courses	Most important reason			Second most important reason			Most or second most important reason		
	GB	Nor	Sp	GB	Nor	Sp	GB	Nor	Sp
Did not have time	24	14	42	16	14	15	39	28	57
Not interested	21	19	15	16	13	16	37	32	30
Felt no need to learn more	13	8	3	12	13	6	25	21	9
Health reasons/feeling too old	12	15	8	7	6	6	20	21	15
Care obligations	9	9	9	5	7	12	14	17	21
There was no suitable course	5	12	4	6	11	6	11	23	10
Too exhausting	3	6	6	6	8	12	9	14	18
Difficult getting time off work	3	2	3	5	4	7	9	6	11
Too expensive	4	5	2	5	5	3	9	10	5
Did not believe I could manage	1	0	2	4	1	3	6	2	5
Found it hard to leave my job	2	2	3	2	3	6	3	6	9
Too far to travel	1	2	2	3	7	2	4	9	4
Did not have the required qualifications	1	1	1	4	3	2	5	4	3
Lacked the necessary skills/abilities	1	0	1	4	0	2	4	1	3
Worried about going out alone	1	0	0	2	1	0	3	1	0
Requirements for reading and writing skills too tough	0	1	0	1	1	1	1	2	1
Did not want to be in a group with people I did not know	0	1	0	1	1	0	1	2	0
Language difficulties	0	0	0	0	1	0	0	1	1
Total	101	97	101	103	99	99	200	200	202

Note: Total will not always be 100 or 200 due to rounding of decimals

8.2 Categories of barriers

As well as evaluating the most important and second most important reasons for non-participation in adult education courses, the Norwegian respondents were also asked to evaluate the significance of each of the 19 barriers (see above). This made it possible to analyse the responses in the Norwegian sample using factor analyses. Used in this context, factor analyses are based on the assumption that behind a number of concrete barriers, a more general barrier factor may be found. From this assumption, the 19 concrete barriers can be reduced to a smaller number of barrier factors (see explanation and justification of factor analyses in chapter five).

The preliminary analyses showed that two of the barriers did not fit well into any factor pattern. These were *there was no suitable course* and *too expensive*. Lack of courses (*there was no suitable course*) was associated most strongly with lack of interest. We felt nonetheless that there were conceptual difference between lack of desire or motivation for participation and a lack of available courses. *Too expensive* was not clearly associated with any of the other barriers. These two barriers were therefore treated as isolated barriers in the further analyses.

The remaining 17 barriers were grouped into six barrier factors, which are shown in table 22 (the pattern matrix is shown in appendix 10). We have called the six barrier factors: *low mastery expectations, social insecurity, work commitments, lack of energy, lack of time* and *lack of motivation*. Table 29 shows the concrete barriers which form each of the barrier factors.

Table 22 Categories of barriers (factor analysis of Norwegian data).

Factors		Statement
Factor 1:	Low mastery expectations (alpha = .80)	Lacked the necessary skills/abilities Did not believe I could manage Requirements for reading and writing skills too tough Did not have the required qualifications Language difficulties
Factor 2:	Social insecurity (alpha = .70)	Worried about going out alone Did not want to be in a group with people I did not know My family did not want me to
Factor 3:	Work commitments (alpha = .82)	Found it hard to leave my job Difficult getting time off work
Factor 4:	Lack of energy (alpha = .55)	Too exhausting Health reasons/feeling too old Too far to travel
Factor 5:	Lack of time (alpha = .55)	Care obligations Did not have time
Factor 6:	Lack of motivation (alpha = .61)	Felt no need to learn more Not interested

8.3 The relative importance of the categories

The main categories of barriers which were found in the Norwegian material were used as a basis for the further analysis of barriers. In order to analyse the significance of the different categories of barriers, we calculated the proportion of respondents who gave one of the barriers which belong to each category as the most important barrier. This can be illustrated using an example. *Care obligations* and *did not have time* comprise the barrier factor *lack of time*. *Care obligations* were identified as the most important barrier by 9.4 % in the Norwegian material while *lack of time* was identified as the most important barrier by 14.2 % of the Norwegian respondents. The barrier factor *lack of time*, which comprises these two barriers, was therefore the most important barrier for 23.6 % of the Norwegian respondents. Similar calculations were carried out for all the barrier factors and for all three countries.

Table 23 shows the significance of each of the barrier factors by showing the proportion of those who did not participate and who gave each barrier factor as the most important barrier. Three of the barrier factors stood out as the most important in all the countries. These concern *lack of energy, lack of time* and *lack of motivation*. The most important barrier belongs to one of these barrier factors for 82 % of non-participants in the British sample, 74 % in the Norwegian sample and 83 % in the Spanish sample. The three main categories of barriers were relatively equally important in the Norwegians sample, while *lack of time* was the most important barrier in the Spanish sample. In the British sample, two of the barrier categories stood out as being the most important. These were *lack of time* and *lack of motivation*.

Table 23 Main barrier factors. Percentage of respondents who indicate each of the factors as the main barrier factor. Base = all non-participants in courses.

	Great Britain N = 908	Norway N = 542	Spain N = 1291
Low mastery expectations	3	3	4
Social insecurity	1	1	0
Work commitments	5	4	7
Lack of energy	16	23	16
Lack of time	32	24	50
Lack of motivation	34	28	17
High costs	4	5	2
No suitable course	5	12	4
Total	**100**	**100**	**100**

The three other barrier factors seemed less significant in the extent that they formed the most important barriers for only 8 – 11 % of those who had not participated. Obviously, this does not mean that these barriers are without significance. On the contrary, for the respondents who report low mastery expectations and social insecurity as the most important barriers against participation, it is anticipated that these will be a major problem. Describing these barriers as less significant simply means that in this case they do not affect so many of the respondents.

The two isolated barriers, which did not fit into any of the barrier factors, were not without significance. Together they form the most important barrier for 17 % of non-participants in the Norwegian sample, but had less significance in Great Britain and in Spain.

8.4 Barriers in subgroups

The most important barriers can, in principle, vary from group to group. As a result, we will look in more depth at barrier factors for men and women, different age groups and respondents with different levels of education. In addition we will look at barrier factors in relation to self-confidence, intrinsic interest value of learning and extrinsic utility value of learning.

Appendix 11 shows the distribution of the most important barrier factors for different groups of non-participants. The three most important general barriers, *lack of energy, lack of time* and *lack of motivation*, appeared to be the most important both for women and for men. The most conspicuous part of the result was that the pattern concerning barriers was very similar for men and women. Nonetheless, the results show that there are clear gender differences regarding these barrier factors. For men, motivational barriers are more important than for women ,while lack of time is stronger for women than for men. The difference in lack of time is however partly compensated for in that work obligations are the most important barriers for more men than for women.

Appendix 11 shows major age differences where barrier factors are concerned. Lack of energy is not an important barrier factor for the youngest respondents, but in all countries it has increasing significance with increased age. Lack of motivation also increases with increased age. For both these barrier factors, the difference between the youngest and oldest age groups is large. The same is true for lack of time. This is a barrier factor which reduces in significance with increasing age. This barrier factor is, however, reduced at a later time in Spain than in the two other countries. In Spain, this barrier factor does not reduce significantly before the age of 60.

The three most important barrier factors were also the most important for respondents at all levels of education. Thus the main pattern of barrier factors is found at all levels of education. However lack of energy was a much stronger barrier for respondents with low levels of education than for respondents with high levels of education. Lack of time increased with increased levels of education in Norway, but was relatively unaffected by level of education in the other countries, while lack of motivation was not related to level of education.

As expected, lack of time was a far more important barrier factor for respondents in employment than for pensioners and those on benefit, who put greater emphasis on *lack of motivation* and *lack of energy*. This is not surprising, since *lack of motivation* and *lack of energy* dominate amongst older respondents and lack of time dominates amongst the youngest. People not working and not seeking work also experienced lack of energy and lack of time as major barrier factors. This may be due to the fact that this group includes a large proportion of people caring for young children.

Appendix 12 shows barriers in relation to self-confidence, intrinsic interest value of learning and extrinsic utility value of learning. A reminder may be useful about what these variable stand for. This is because self-confidence can be regarded as another form of low mastery expectations and of social insecurity, while intrinsic and extrinsic utility value of learning can be seen as an alternative indication of motivation. It should be remembered that self-confidence, intrinsic interest value and extrinsic utility value of learning were general measures of self-perception, values and attitudes, and were not measured with reference to participation in adult education; while low mastery expectations, social insecurity and lack of motivation were registered as the respondents' own evaluation of the reasons for non-participation on courses.

Somewhat surprisingly, the barriers of *low mastery expectations* and *social insecurity* were not systematically related to self-confidence. This means that people with low self-confidence do not report low mastery expectations regarding education or social insecurity as barriers to a greater degree than others. All the three dominant barrier factors were, however, systematically related to the perceived value of learning. The "lack of motivation" barrier was strongest amongst respondents with low intrinsic and extrinsic value of learning. This illustrates that a general lack of perceived (intrinsic or extrinsic) value of learning manifest itself as conscious reasons for not participating in adult education. This can be regarded as a validation of the respondents' statement. At the same time, it gives reason to raise the question of the use of the barrier concept surrounding these reasons for non-participation in education. The barrier factor *lack of energy* was strongest among respondents with low extrinsic value of learning.

8.5 Comments

Respondents who had not participated in adult education during the last three years evaluated 19 potential reasons for their non-participation. As well as stating the most important reason for non-participation, they evaluated the significance of each of the 19 reasons. We will provisionally describe the 19 reasons as obstacles or barriers.

Factor analysis of the Norwegian data revealed that the 19 barriers could be grouped in six categories of barriers plus two isolated barriers. The six barrier factors were: *low mastery expectations, social insecurity, work obligations, lack of energy, lack of time* and *lack of motivation*. The two isolated barriers were: *no suitable course* and *high cost*.

The barrier factors will obviously depend on the concrete barriers identified by the respondents. The six barrier factors should not therefore be construed as the only possible barrier factors. On the other hand, it is important that these barriers are taken into account in planning and working in adult education. When we found two isolated barriers, this may also be seen as a result of the barriers identified by the respondents. If we had presented more barriers focusing course opportunities and costs, there is every reason to believe that these two areas would also have appeared as barrier factors (main groups of barriers).

This consideration leads to eight barrier factors which can be grouped into four intrinsic or psychological factors and four extrinsic or environmental factors. The four intrinsic factors are:

lack of motivation
low mastery expectations
social insecurity
lack of energy

Here it can be argued that lack of energy is in fact an intrinsic barrier, but one that cannot be described as psychological. Our argument is that the conditions which go into this barrier factor - feelings of being too old and expectations that participation will be too tiring - are relative evaluations which are strongly related to motivation and self-image. It also appears that three of the psychological barrier factors, *low mastery expectations, social insecurity* and *lack of energy* correlate positively with each other.

If we assume that behind the two isolated barriers there also lie barrier factors, we can point out four external barrier factors:

work obligations
lack of time
no suitable course
high costs.

In principal, these are external, environmental barrier factors. However, these conditions are also the subject of a subjective evaluation. Clear delineation between intrinsic and extrinsic barriers can therefore be difficult to establish.

Three of the barrier factors stand out as being of particular significance. These barriers were *lack of motivation, lack of energy* and *lack of time*. The three most significant barrier factors are almost zero-correlated. That is to say they appeared as central, independent barrier factors. This again means that work to reduce or remove these barriers must be done separately, related to each barrier factor. Reduction of one of these factors will have little significance for the other two.

Two of the three most important barrier factors were intrinsic, psychological factors. In Great Britain and Norway these categories were the main reason for not participating for circa half of all respondents who had not participated in adult education in the previous three years. This shows the great significance of psychological conditions in participation in adult education. At the same time it raises an important question on how meaningful it is to talk about obstacles or barriers. Seen from the provider's viewpoint, lack of motivation can be seen as a barrier, at least if the aim is for as many people as possible to participate in courses as often as possible. From the employer's point of view, the evaluation may be the same, because participation is viewed from the perspective of the person or persons who benefit from others taking courses. Seen from the perspective of the individual, on the other hand, it is less meaningful to characterise lack of motivation as a barrier. In order for an individual to have a barrier, he or she must first have a goal or a desire. If one person's goal runs contrary to participating in adult education, this can hardly be seen as a barrier for the person himself.

Low mastery expectations and social insecurity are also psychological reasons for non-participation. These are psychological reasons for non-participation which can easily be characterised as barriers. These are reasons which we find both amongst respondents who are motivated and respondents who are not motivated to participate. We have shown that these barriers are only significant for smaller groups of respondents. Nonetheless they must be taken seriously, because they are barriers which are difficult to reduce. As a result they may become insurmountable barriers for some people.

In spite of the general tendency towards lack of time, energy and motivation being the most important reasons for non-participation in adult education for the majority of the subgroups in our sample, we found important group differences. It may be particularly interesting to look more closely at some of the subgroups who have a low participation frequency. This concerns the oldest and those with the lowest levels of education in particular. For both these groups, *lack of energy* was a far more important barrier factor than for the youngest and those with higher education. In other words, adults with low levels of education and older adults have more intrinsic, psychological barriers than young adults and adults with higher levels of education. For the last group, it is first and foremost lack of time which is the dominant barrier factor

Adults with low perceived intrinsic or extrinsic value of learning stated lack of motivation as a reason for not participating in adult education to a far greater extent than others. This is only to be expected. This means that the general attitude towards learning manifests itself in concrete situations, also connected to adult education. This illustrates a relation between general attitudes, values and actual behaviour (for example choices between different activities).

Adults with low self-confidence and low extrinsic value of learning stood out in that they stated lack of energy as the most important reason for not participating in adult education to a much greater extent than others did. As stated, low self-confidence can lead to both anxiety and the need for self –protection strategies and therefore be energy -demanding (S. Skaalvik, 1999). This can lead to insecurity regarding one's own ability to master given situations (Covington, 1992). Low self-confidence can also lead to the need to avoid negative evaluations in the environment and to hide the problems. Different strategies for self protection may be adopted (see Breakwell, 1986; Covington, 1992; Rosenberg, 1979). Both the anxiety and the self-protection strategies demand energy and can partially explain why adults with low self-confidence state lack of energy as an important barrier.

9 ADULTS' LEARNING STRATEGIES

Adults can adopt different strategies for learning something new. If somebody is going to learn something new about a subject, there are different ways to approach it. Some choose to go on an organised course with personal meetings. Others will look for information and try to learn on their own. Others may ask someone else for advice or guidance. Others will undertake distance learning, either by following teaching on the radio or television, through a correspondence course or by using the Internet

In this study, we tried to obtain answers to the following questions:

- Is the choice of learning strategy connected with the type of subject one wishes to learn about?
- Is the choice of learning strategy dependent on what one already knows about the subject?
- Does the choice of learning strategy vary with age, gender and education ?

9.1 Choosing learning subjects

We selected in advance some subjects or areas which the respondents might wish to learn more about. The subjects chosen were: 1) cookery, 2) computers 3) employment law 4) foreign languages. The subjects were selected to cover both practical and more theoretical areas. The purpose was to find subjects where the participants had relatively good prior knowledge and other subjects where many had little prior experience. In addition, the respondents had the opportunity to express their opinion about a subject they had chosen themselves which they wished to learn more about.

9.2 Self-evaluation of prior knowledge

Individual prior knowledge was not tested. Instead, we asked the respondents themselves to evaluate how well they knew each individual area. This was registered on a four-point scale. Different people probably have different criteria for what represents a lot or a little knowledge of an area. In the first instance, the point was to chart how the respondents *themselves* felt or experienced the knowledge they had. This was to analyse whether the choice of learning strategy was related to the respondents judgements of their prior knowledge and skills in the chosen areas.

9.3 Preferred learning strategies

We will first look at the preferred learning strategies in the different areas. Table 24 shows the four stated learning areas plus a self-selected area (which varies from person to person). The table further shows the percentage of all those asked who preferred each strategy for learning in the area in question.

Table 24 shows that the main strategy for learning was to go to a class. When the subjects to be learned were computing skills, a foreign language or a chosen topic, going to a class was the preferred strategy for 60-80 % of the respondents in all three countries.

However, the choices vary, both between the countries and with the subject to be learned. Going to a class was the main strategy among the Spanish respondents irrespective of the subject to be learned. When the subject to be learned was cookery, only about one in three respondents in Great Britain and Norway preferred to go to a class and equally many preferred to seek information and try it out on their own. Asking for advice was also a common strategy. For learning about employment law and regulations the British respondents deviated from the Norwegian and the Spanish respondents in that the most preferred strategy among the British respondents was to ask somebody they knew for advice and guidance.

Table 24 Percentage who prefer different strategies for learning different topics. Base = all respondents.

Preferred learning strategy	Subject for learning		
	Cookery		
	Great Britain	Norway	Spain
Go to a class	35	34	58
Seek information and try it out on my own	30	35	14
Ask somebody I know for advice and guidance	16	22	19
Watch/listen to TV /radio instruction programmes	17	6	6
Take a correspondence course	1	1	3
Use Internet/modern technology	1	3	1
Total	100	101	101
	Computers		
Go to a class	60	71	78
Seek information and try it out on my own	9	8	7
Ask somebody I know for advice and guidance	18	12	8
Watch/listen to TV/radio instruction programmes	3	2	2
Take a correspondence course	5	1	3
Use Internet/modern technology	5	6	2
Total	100	100	100
	Employment law		
Go to a class	25	51	68
Seek information and try it out on my own	17	17	13
Ask somebody I know for advice and guidance	41	18	12
Watch/listen to TV/radio instruction programmes	6	3	2
Take a correspondence course	6	6	4
Use Internet/modern technology	5	6	1
Total	100	101	100
	Foreign language		
Go to a class	69	62	80
Seek information and try it out on my own	7	16	6
Ask somebody I know for advice and guidance	6	4	6
Watch/listen to TV/radio instruction programmes	7	7	2
Take a correspondence course	10	7	4
Use Internet/modern technology	2	4	1
Total	101	100	99
	Chosen topic		
Go to a class	74	84	80
Seek information and try it out on my own	7	6	9
Ask somebody I know for advice and guidance	5	5	5
Watch/listen to TV/radio instruction programmes	5	1	2
Take a correspondence course	7	3	3
Use Internet/modern technology	3	2	1
Total	101	101	100

NOTE: total varies from 100 to 101 due to rounding of decimals

It is also worth noting that very few respondents chose strategies which involve the use of radio, TV, correspondence courses or the Internet. This occurs independently of the subject to be learned, including learning about computers. One exeption however, is learning cookery in Great Britain, where as much as 17 percent would prefer to learn from radio or TV. Still, confidence in distance learning and the Internet as teaching tools does not yet appear to be very strong. In the eagerness to adopt new technological media for use in teaching, it should be noted the majority of people are not yet familiar with the type of learning processes which these entail.

The results correspond well with an earlier Norwegian study by Skaalvik & Knudsen (1979). In this study, people were asked, amongst other things, about the method they would prefer to learn more about the subjects of food preparation, English and law in everyday life. Around 60 to 70 % chose to go to a class as a strategy for learning in these areas. Here, we should point out that in this study we have given a wide definition of adult education as all forms of organised learning. In connection with questions on learning strategies, we have nonetheless made a distinction between "going to a class" and different types of distance education, for example correspondence courses, which are also organised forms of learning. Nonetheless such large support for "going to a class" indicates a relatively traditional understanding of teaching as well as learning.

The differences in strategic choice depending on the theme can be interpreted in several ways. One possible interpretation is that practical activities are easier to learn on one's own than more theoretical knowledge. It is therefore not so necessary to go to a class to learn more about food preparation. Yet use of computers requires practical skills. Another possible interpretation is that areas which appear to be complicated are seen as areas where it is best to learn by going to a class, with a teacher or leader with whom one can meet and talk. A third possibility is that people have a tendency to choose going to a class as a form of learning when they have little prior knowledge of the subject. We will look more closely at this last possible interpretation.

9.4 The significance of prior knowledge in the choice of learning strategies

As stated above, the respondents were asked to evaluate their own knowledge in the four areas. Table 25 shows the percentage of respondents who chose to go to classes, divided into those who felt they knew a lot about the subject and those who knew little about the subject. The results shows no systematic tendencies in any of the countries towards a systematic relation between prior knowledge and choice of learning strategy. The picture we obtain is that the difference between those who have good prior knowledge and those who have little prior knowledge is relatively small when it comes to choice of learning strategies. The variation is much greater between subject areas than between groups with different levels prior knowledge within each subject area. Therefore we have no clear indication that the degree of prior knowledge of an area has any significance on the choice of learning strategy. The results indicate rather that it is the perception of the subject itself, and perhaps its degree of complexity, which affect adults' choices of learning strategies.

Table 25 Percentage of the respondents who prefer to go to a class in order to learn different topics, grouped by familiarity with the topic.

Subject for learning	Knowledge about the topic	GB	Nor	Sp
Cookery	Very much or quite a lot	34	35	67
	Very little or little	35	32	55
	Total, cookery	**35**	**34**	**58**
Computers	Very much or quite a lot	52	69	83
	Very little or little	63	73	74
	Total, computers	**60**	**71**	**78**
Employment law and regulations	Very much or quite a lot	23	54	69
	Very little or little	26	47	67
	Total, law and regulations	**25**	**51**	**68**
Foreign language	Very much or quite a lot	61	60	85
	Very little or little	70	67	78
	Total, foreign language	**69**	**62**	**80**
Chosen topic	Very much or quite a lot	68	84	78
	Very little or little	78	85	82
	Total, chosen topic	**74**	**84**	**80**

9.5 Strategies in different subgroups

In table 26a and b, we have concentrated only on those who said they have *little* or *very little* knowledge of the different subjects. We have split these into different subgroups according to gender, age and education. The results do not indicate that the tendency to choose to go to a class to learn something new varies systematically with gender, age or level of education.

Table 26a Percentage in different subgroups who prefer to go to a class in order to learn in different areas. Base = all respondents who say they have little or very little knowledge on each area.

Background variables		Subject for learning					
		Cookery			Computers		
		GB	Norway	Spain	GB	Norway	Spain
		N = 580	N = 558	N = 1358	N = 1077	N = 970	N = 1117
Gender	Men	34	34	55	60	72	74
	Women	37	27	56	65	75	74
Age	18-29	23	20	56	64	75	71
	30-45	36	35	55	68	77	73
	46-59	39	44	59	65	75	78
	60-79	41	36	53	55	65	72
Level of education	No formal	40	-	58	58	-	74
	Primary/lower sec.	35	31	56	69	66	74
	Upper secondary	30	31	55	68	77	70
	College/university	32	36	54	64	72	74

9.6 Comments

The study shows that going to a class is the preferred learning strategy for most adults who want to learn more about a specific subject. Nonetheless, the choice of strategy varies with the choice of subject. Of the subjects we chose to asked the respondents about, food preparation, stood out as a subject where the majority in Great Britain and Norway chose strategies other than going to a class.

Table 26b Percentage in different subgroups who prefer to go to a class in order to learn in different areas. Base = all respondents who say they have little or very little knowledge on each area.

		Subject for learning							
		Employment law			Foreign language			Chosen topic		
		GB	Nor	Sp	GB	Nor	Sp	GB	Nor	Sp
Background variables		N = 955	N = 879	N = 1308	N = 1289	N = 633	N = 1249	N = 450	N = 589	N = 349
Gender	Men	28	50	67	65	65	79	71	82	77
	Women	25	45	68	74	69	78	83	88	86
Age	18-29	15	46	66	71	71	82	86	85	85
	30-45	25	50	63	73	70	78	79	89	84
	46-59	31	48	74	65	68	79	71	81	85
	60-79	31	44	68	69	61	75	79	82	66
Level of education	No formal	36	-	71	65	-	77	77	-	78
	Primary/lower sec.	22	48	68	71	62	78	81	81	83
	Upper secondary	28	46	66	77	72	80	89	85	85
	College/university	15	52	62	74	60	80	72	86	74

The degree of prior knowledge about the subjects appears to have little effect on whether one chooses to go to a class rather than adopting other strategies. Choosing to go to a class as a learning strategy does also not vary systematically with gender, age or level of education.

The differences in participation in adult education over the last three years and in probable participation in the future which we have found between younger and older people, and between the different educational groups, cannot be explained through different tendencies for preferring to go to a class as a strategy for learning something new. It appears therefore that the difference in participation between young and old and between respondents with different levels of education must be explained in other ways. The results of this study rather indicate that these groups stand out from each other with regard to motivation, and opportunities to take part in adult learning.

10 SUMMARY AND DISCUSSION

10.1 The scale of adult education and description of the courses

Both the scale and the pattern of adult education varies largely between the three countries involved in the MOBA project. Over a three year period the proportion of adults who have participated in adult education was almost twice as high in Norway as in Great Britain and Spain. Whereas 70 % of the Norwegian sample had participated in adult education, corresponding figures in Spain and Great Britain were 32 % and 41 %, respectively. However, the volume of adult education at a given point in time, measured in the number of adults participating, were very similar in all three countries.

The pattern of adult education varies greatly between the countries. The adult education in Norway was dominated by relatively short, but high time-consuming work-related courses, whereas the adult education in Spain was more characterised by longer academic courses. In contrast, adult learning in Great Britain was dominated by less intensive courses which varied both with respect to content and duration, but also with work-related courses as the dominant type of adult education. In Great Britain and Norway the tendency was also that those who had participated in work-related courses had done more than one course during the last three years. Because this was not true for other type of courses it further illustrates the dominant position of work-related adult education.

An important difference between the countries was also that participation took place during work hours far more frequently in Great Britain and Norway than in Spain. The Spanish respondents were also less confident that they could get time off from work in order to follow courses than the respondents in Great Britain and Norway. These differences in opportunities of doing courses at the work place or during work hours may partly explain the differences between the countries in participation in adult education.

A comparison of the Norwegian results with previous Norwegian surveys reveal that it is work-related adult education that has increased the most during the last 20 years. Thus, work-related adult education gradually has come to constitute a larger part of the total adult education. This may partly be explained by the fact that in Norway most young adults graduate from high school. The need for general and academic adult education is therefore diminished. It may also partly be explained by the increasing need for readjustment in business life and therefore for individual workers to continuously increase and renew their competence. We may predict that a similar development has taken place in Great Britain and will take place in Spain.

10.2 Who takes part in adult education?

Previous surveys are inconsistent with respect to differences in participation among men and women. However, Norwegian surveys show that men take part in work-related courses more than women, while women participate more than men in other types of courses. The MOBA study shows only small and negligible differences between men and women in participation. However, in all three countries a somewhat greater proportion of men had participated in vocational and work-related courses compared to women whereas larger proportion of women than men participate in recreational and leisure courses.

The results reveal greater differences between various age groups. As could be expected, the youngest respondents (between 18 and 29) participated far more in general and academic courses than any other age group. For these type of courses participation drops dramatically after the age of 30. The picture looks different for other types of courses, where the participation rate did not differ much between the early twenties and the late fifties in Great Britain and Norway, but dropped steeply after the mid forties in Spain. Comparing these results with previous Norwegian studies reveal that the relation between age and participation has changed over time.

In all three countries respondents with low levels of education participate to a relatively small extent in adult education, while participants with higher levels of education participate most. For all three countries there is a relatively dramatic increase in participation when the level of education of the respondents is above elementary school level. Whereas this could be expected for general and academic courses it was also evident for work-related courses. A very important task for follow up studies is to further explore reasons for the relation between level of education and participation in work-related adult education. An important reason indicated in this study is that the possibility of getting time off from work to attend adult education increases strongly with increased level of education. Therefore, combating exclusion from the labour marked through adult education is not only a matter of personal motivation, but is also a question of attitude and policy at the workplace.

A firm conclusion that can be based on the present study is that psychological variables like self-confidence and perceived value of learning are important determinants for participation in adult education. Still, these variables had a somewhat different impact on participation in the three countries. A common feature was that extrinsic utility value of learning strongly influenced participation in all countries. However, intrinsic interest value of learning had a strong impact on participation in Great Britain and Spain, whereas self-confidence was strongly related to participation only in Spain. It is important to note that these tendencies were found irrespective of gender, age, and level of education. We can only speculate about the difference between the countries. One possible interpretation may be based on the general level of education and the scale of adult education in the three countries. We find the lowest level of education in the Spanish sample where a large majority lacks educational experiences after leaving primary school. This may explain why low self-confidence has such a large effect on participation in adult education. Possible explanations of the Norwegian result may be that the scale of participation is very high in Norway, that the level of education is high and that a large majority of the courses are work- related and take place during working hours. Both the high level of education and the high rate of participation may result in a strong belief that continuous education is important, which may overshadow the impact of both self-confidence and intrinsic interest value of learning.

10.3 Motivation for participation

Respondents who had participated in education the last three years were given 14 potential motives for participating. Factor analysis of the Norwegian data revealed that 10 of the reasons formed three identifiable motivational factors or categories of motives: *personal development, new work situation, and carrying out one's work better*. Analyses of the responses in all countries were based on these categories of motives.

Work-related motives were the most important motives for the majority of participants. Seen together, work-related motives were the most important motivation for participating for 62 %, 64 %, and 72 % of the respondents from Great Britain, Norway, and Spain, respectively. However, for participants in Great Britain and Norway the most important work-related motive was to improve one's skills in order to perform one's work better. In contrast, for participants in Spain the most important work- related motive was to get a job, get a new job, or to change one's work situation.

Even though work- related motives dominated, personal development was the main reason for participating for 20-24 % of the respondents in all countries. Moreover, it was the second most important motive for another 40-45 % of the respondents in all countries. Thus, personal development is an important additional motive for a majority of respondents who have work-related main reasons for participating. This is a very important result, because it indicates that the change in adult education towards more work-related learning may not have reduced participants' desire for the learning to result in personal development. In fact, it may often be the joint effect of work-related motives and motivation for personal development that leads to the decision to participate in education.

The percentage of the respondents who regarded it likely or very likely that they would participate in courses the next three years corresponded closely with the actual participation in the previous three years. An interesting observation was that the majority of those who had participated in the last three years also considered it possible that they would participate in the next three years. By way of comparison, only between 20 and 30 per cent of those who had not participated in the last three years regarded participation as probable in the next period. We have given different possible interpretations of this finding. One possible interpretation is that those who have participated feel that the rewards have been great, and that they therefore wish to participate in the future. Such an interpretation corresponds well with the rather positive evaluations of the benefits of the courses given by the participants. An alternative, but not conflicting interpretation, can be based on the fact that the great majority of participants had taken part in courses which were related to their work and which to a large extent took place during working hours. The result can then be interpreted to show that those who had such opportunities previously are in positions in their working life where they feel that similar opportunities will be available in the future. There is every reason to look at this interpretation more closely in research projects which are designed for this purpose, since it also implies that a number of employees have few opportunities for education and increasing their competence at their workplace. The results further indicate that this may be particularly true for employees with low level of education.

10.4 Benefits of adult education

The respondents were asked to indicate the benefit of the last course by responding to 13 statements about benefit. We then looked at benefits judged to be useful or very useful by at least 60 % of the participants. This procedure revealed major differences between the countries. In Norway, where the scale of participation was the highest, the perceived benefit of the courses was the lowest, or was narrowed down to a few aspects of benefit. By comparison, in Spain, where the scale of participation was the lowest, the perceived benefit was the highest, with a broad range of perceived benefits.

These seemingly paradoxical results are discussed from both a motivational and a planning point of view. Norway is approaching a situation where most adults, at least at some point, are involved in some kind of formal learning - particularly at the workplace. Seen from a participant's perspective, this may mean that participation in adult education has become so commonplace that participation does not always build on any strong motivation or is followed by any great input. In the worst case, learning at work may simply have become a welcome change from work itself. In Spain we have seen that participation in adult education is much lower. This is particularly true for learning at the workplace. This may mean that interest in participation is much greater than the opportunities for participating, and motivation and input among those who participate may therefore be greater. However, the result can also be interpreted from a provider perspective. With the expansion of adult education in Norway, the demand has become great. Many courses are planned and arranged, and great financial interest is connected with the implementation of courses. The question arises whether the tempo has become too fast to ensure sufficient attention to quality assurance. Where participation is lower, for example in Spain, quality assurance of the courses can thus be given greater attention.

These processes may well work together. It is possible that when both the scale of and the demand for adult education increases, then there is a risk that the quality of the education offered is reduced whereas the participants' expectations of and demand for quality increases. Therefore, as the scale of adult education steadily increases, there is a need to look more closely at the quality of the education offered.

10.5 Barriers

The participants in the study responded to 19 possible barriers, which were classified into six barrier factors and two separate barriers: *lack of motivation, low mastery expectations, social insecurity, lack of energy, work obligations, lack of time, no suitable course, and high costs.* The first four of these were regarded as "psychological barriers".

Three of the barrier factors stood out as the most important in all the countries. These were *lack of energy, lack of time* and *lack of motivation*. The single most important barrier belongs to one of these factors for 82 % of non- participants in the British sample, 74 % in the Norwegian sample and 83 % in the Spanish sample.

The three main categories of barriers were relatively equally important in the Norwegians sample. In the British sample, two of the barrier categories stood out as being the most important. These were *lack of time* and *lack of motivation. Lack of time* was the most important barrier in the Spanish sample and was perceived as far more important than in the two other samples. The reason for this is probably a combination of the organisation of the working day in Spain and the fact that the respondents in the Spanish sample perceived the possibility of getting time off from work to do courses as much smaller than respondents in Great Britain and Norway.

The three most significant barrier factors are almost zero-correlated. That is to say they appeared as central, independent obstacle factors. This again means that work to reduce or remove these barriers must be done separately and that reduction of one of these factors will have little significance for the other two.

10.6 Adults' learning strategies

Preferred learning strategies were in this study explored by presenting to the respondents four subjects or topics for learning and asking for the preferred way of going about learning (more) about the topics. The study shows that going to a class is the preferred learning strategy for most adults who want to learn more about a specific subject. Furthermore, choosing to go to a class as a learning strategy does not vary systematically with gender, age or level of education. More importantly, the degree of prior knowledge about the subjects appears to have little effect on whether one chooses to go to a class rather than adopting other strategies.

The differences in participation over the last three years and in probable participation in the future which we have found between younger and older people, and between the different educational groups, cannot be explained through different tendencies for preferring to go to a class as a strategy for learning something new. It appears therefore that the difference in participation between young and old and between respondents with different levels of education must be explained in other ways. The results of this study rather indicate that these groups stand out from each other with regard to motivation, perception of the value of learning, and opportunities to take part in adult learning which exist or which are perceived to exist at the work place.

10.7 A model for participation in adult education

In this survey we have concentrated on participation in adult education with special focus on the scale of participation, who participates, motives for participation and barriers or reasons for not participating. The research was based on an implicit model of participation. The model, which is shown in figure 2, gives a more complete picture of adult education than can be explored in a single survey. We shall therefore both comment on the model in general and in relation to the results of this study.

In the model we consider that participation is a result of the individual's desire or motivation to participate, stimulation or pressure from the immediate environment to participate, and different forms of obstacles or barriers. Desires and psychological barriers are affected by a person's values, interests, self-perception, attitudes, needs and expectations, but also by the opportunities or lack of opportunities for adult education. The psychological processes are again influenced by general social and cultural conditions such as prevailing values and norms, economic conditions in society and developments in the work force, but also in relation to a person's immediate environment. The psychological processes are also influenced by previous experiences and current life situations. Participation in adult education provides further experiences which can alter or strengthen the psychological processes such as the participant's interests and expectations.

This project has only looked at selected aspects of the model. We have only briefly pointed out some social and cultural conditions which differ between the countries. The development in working life and the rhetoric of the knowledge-based society have contributed towards creating a general feeling of a need for a continual increase in competence. The development of adult education towards a steadily stronger dominance of work-related training, that we particularly find in Great Britain and Norway, must be seen in this context. We anticipate a similar development in adult education in Spain during the next decades. At present, external barriers, particularly lack of time, seem to be the most important barriers against participation. These external barriers must be interpreted in terms of the respondents life situation.

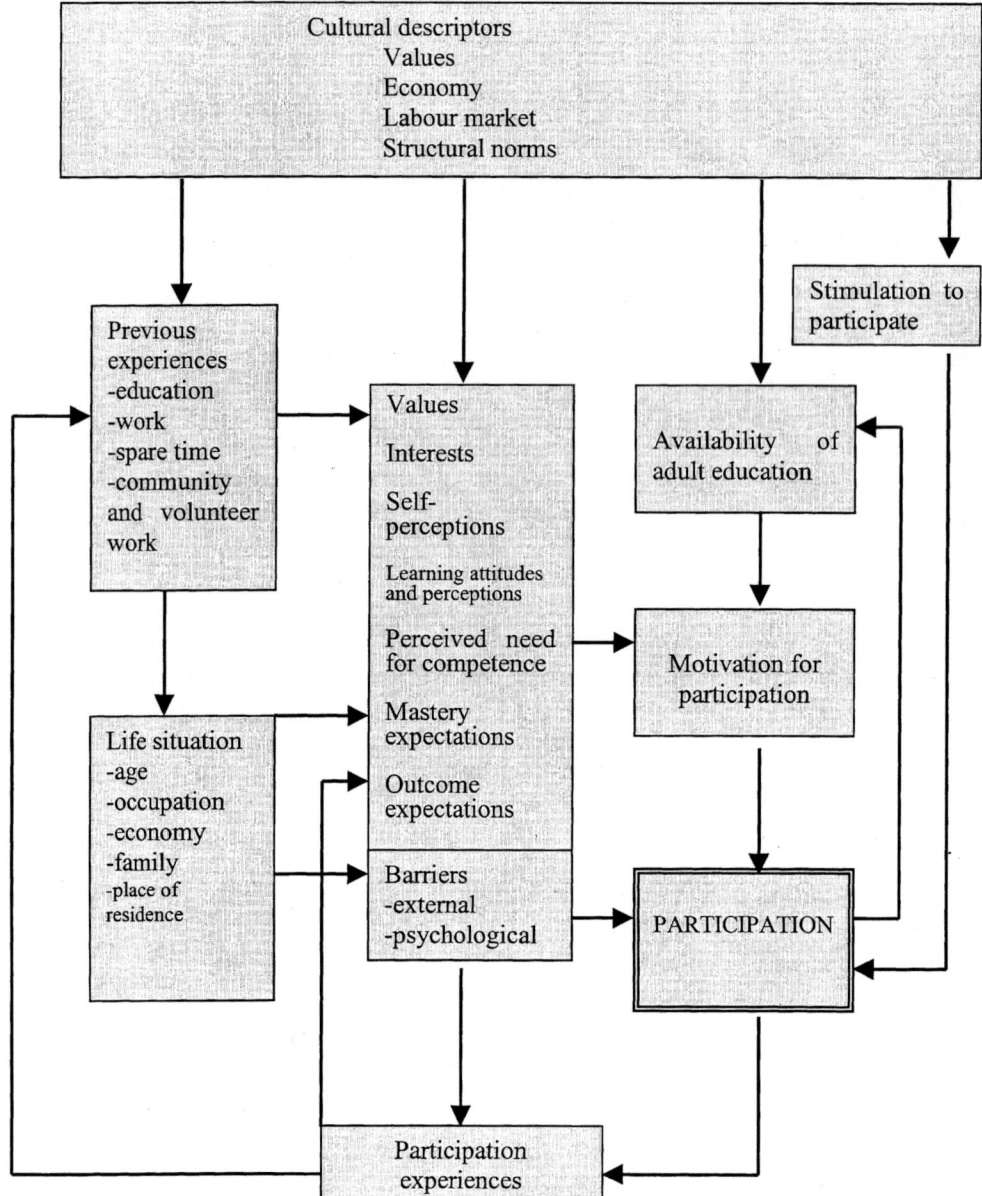

Figure 2 A model for participation in adult education

The model is based on the fact that previous experiences are partly the result of social and cultural conditions, such as the school system, the prevailing working methods and the forms of assessment which exist. The experiences in their turn form a basis for values, interests, self-perceptions, perceived value of learning etc. In the present survey, previous experiences have been observed in terms of both the respondents' general level of education and their prior experiences of participating in adult education. The research shows that in all countries both the level of education and prior experience with adult education are strongly related to both participation and the desire to participate in the future. The results further show that the impact of previous experiences is partly mediated via a perceived need for education (extrinsic utility value of learning). This illustrates that previous experiences are significant for the psychological process (such as interest and perceived value of learning) which again have an effect on participation.

Participation in adult education creates new experiences. These experiences then become "previous experiences" with the significance this has for the psychological processes. It means that the people who organise adult education are also contributors to the complicated process which is decisive for later participation.

The figure shows a model for participation in adult education with the main emphasis on the question of recruitment. It could be expanded by including processes related to participation itself. Important questions would then be related to teaching and working methods, how the content fits the participants' needs and expectations, to what degree education is followed by a feeling of mastery and in what way the participants later use their increased competence. These are particularly important questions for further research within adult education. Since our research focuses on these questions to a small extent, we have not included such conditions in the model.

The results we have obtained correspond well with the model. However, the model includes far more than is shown by our data. The model can therefore function as a starting point for future research by indicating conditions upon which research should throw more light.

Even though the general model in figure 2 fits well with the data from all countries, adult education at the start of the new millennium differs considerably between the countries involved in this study. The differences are most clearly observed regarding the scale of adult education, aims and motives for participation, possibility of taking time off from work to engage in education, educational possibilities at the workplace, perceived benefit of adult education and barriers. The problems and the challenges therefore are different and may have to be addressed in different ways.

A common challenge for all countries is to provide more equal opportunities to engage in learning at the workplace, irrespective of gender, age and level of education. Employees with low levels of education do not frequently take part in work-related courses. A question arising from this is how these employees are dealt with and how they learn new skills at their work. To some extent this is a question of whether equal opportunities for participation in courses are given, but it is also a question if alternative ways of learning than signing up for courses are provided. There is a need to explore to what degree such models are in use and how they work. Alternatively, it is a task for the field of adult education research to develop alternative models for learning.

REFERENCES

Bandura, A. (1986). *Social Foundations of Thought and Action: A Social Cognitive Theory.*

Beder, H.W. and Valentine, T. (1990). Motivational profiles of adult basic education students. *Adult Education Quarterly, 40,* 78-94.

Boshier, R. (1977). Motivational orientations re-visited: life space motives and education participation scale. *Adult Education, 27,* 89-115.

Boshier, R. (1991). Psychometric properties of the alternative form of the education participation scale. *Adult Education Quarterly, 41,* 150-167.

Breakwell, G.M. (1986). *Cooping with threatened identities.* London: Methuen.

Covington, M.V. (1992). *Making the grade: A self-worth perspective on motivation and school reform.* Cambridge: University Press.

Cross, K.P. (1981). *Adults as learners.* San Francisco: Jossey-Bass.

Darkenwald, G.G. and Valentine, T. (1985). Factor structure of deterrents to public participation in adult education. *Adult Education Quarterly, 35,* 177-193.

Deci, E. and Ryan, R. (1985). *Intrinsic motivation and self-determination in human behavior.* New York: Plenum.

Eccles, J. (1987). Gender roles and achievement patterns: an expectancy value perspective. In J.M. Reinisch, L.A. Rosenblum, and S.A. Sanders (Eds.), *Masculinity/femininity: Basic perspectives* (pp. 240-280). New York: Oxford University Press.

FOREM (2000). *Motivaciones y barreras para la participación en la educación de adultos.* Madrid: Fundación Formación y empleo Miguel Escalera. FOREM.

Hackett, G. (1995). Self-efficacy in career choice and development. In A. Bandura (Ed.), *Self-efficacy in changing societies* (pp. 232-258). New York: Cambridge University Press.

Hackett, G., Betz, N.E., O'Halloran, M.S. and Romac, D.S. (1990). Effects of verbal and mathematics task performance on task and career self-efficacy and interest. *Journal of Counceling Psychology,* 37, 169-177.

Hillage, J., Uden, T., Aldridge, F. and Eccles, J. (2000). *Adult Learning in England: a review.* IES Report 369. Brighton: Institute for Employment Studies (IES) and National Institute of Adult Continuing Education (NIACE).

Jonstone, J.W.C. and Rivera, R.J. (1965). Volunteers for learning: *A study of the educational pursuits of American adults.* Chicago: Aldine Publishing Company.

Nicholls, J. (1984). Conceptions of ability and achievement motivation. In R. Ames and C. Ames (Eds.), *Research on motivation in education: Vol. 1. Student motivation* (pp. 39-73). New York: Academic Press.

OECD (1998). *Education at a Glance – OECD Indicators.* Paris.

Pajares, F. (1997). Current directions in self-efficacy research. In M.L. Maehr and P.R. Pintrich (Eds.), *Advances in motivation and achievement, Vol. 10* (pp. 1-49). Greenwich, Connecticut: JAI Press.

Pintrich, P.R. and Schunk, D.H. (1996). *Motivation in education : theory, research and applications.* Englewood Cliffs, N.J.: Prentice-Hall.

Rosenberg, M. (1979). *Conceiving the Self.* New York: Basic Books.

Rubenson, K. (1975). *Rekrytering til vuxenutbildning. En studie av kortutbildade yngre män.* Göteborgs Universitet.

Sargant, N. (1991). *Learning & leisure: A study of adult participation in learning and its policy implications.* Leicester: The National Institute of Adult Continuing Education (NIACE).

Sargant, N. (2000). *The learning devide revisited.* Leicester: The National Institute of Adult Continuing Education (NIACE).

Sargant, N., Field, J., Hywel, F., Schuller,T. and Tuckett, A. (1997). *The Learning divide. A study of participation in adult learning in the United Kingdom.* Leicester: The National Institute of Adult Continuing Education (NIACE).

Scanlan, C.L. and Darkenwald, G.G. (1984). Identifying deterrents to participation in continuing education. *Adult Education Quarterly, 34,* 155-166.

Skaalvik, E.M. (1979). *Rekruttering til voksenopplæring.* Trondheim: Norsk voksenpedagogisk institutt.

Skaalvik, E.M. and Engesbak, H. (1996). Selvrealisering og kompetanseutvikling: Rekruttering til voksenopplæring i et tjueårsperspektiv. In S. Tøsse (Ed.), *Fra lov til reform.* (pp. 89-128). Trondheim: Norsk voksenpedagogisk forskningsinstitutt.

Skaalvik, E.M., Finbak, L. and Ljosland, O.-H. (2000). *Voksenopplæring i Norge ved tusenårsskiftet. Deltakelse, motivasjon og barrierer.* Trondheim: Norsk voksenpedagogisk forskningsinstitutt.

Skaalvik, E.M. and Knudsen, K. (1979). *Deltakelse i voksenopplæring. Noen sentrale fordelinger.* Trondheim: Norsk voksenpedagogisk institutt.

Skaalvik, E.M. and Tvete, S. (1980). *Voksenopplæring i Trøndelag: formål, undervisning, deltakervurdering.* Trondheim: Norsk voksenpedagogisk institutt.

Skaalvik, E.M and Skaalvik S. (1993). Selvoppfatning og forventninger: sentrale motivasjonsfaktorer i voksenopplæring. In V. Haugerud and J. Kvam (Eds.), *Livslang læring. En antologi om voksenopplæringens mangfold og enhet.* Trondheim: Norsk voksenpedagogisk forskningsinstitutt.

Skaalvik, S. (1999). *Hverdag, arbeid og utdanning. En studie av voksne med lese- og skrivevansker.* Trondheim: Norsk voksenpedagogisk forskningsinstitutt.

Tuckett, A. and Sargant, N. (1999). *Marking Time.* Leicester: The National Institute of Adult Continuing Education (NIACE).

Tøsse, S. (1998). *Kunnskap til makt. Politisk opplysningsarbeid i norsk arbeidarrørsle frå 1880-åra til 1940.* Trondheim: Norsk vaksenpedagogisk forskningsinstitutt.

Wigfield, A. and Eccles, J.S. (1992). The development of achievement task values: A theoretical analysis. *Developmental Review, 12,* 265-310.

LIST OF FIGURES

Figure 1 Path analysis with probable participation in the next three years as the dependent variable. 33
Figure 2 A model for participation in adult education 58

LIST OF TABLES

Table 1 Motivation factors identified in two surveys (Boshier, 1991; Beder and Valentine, 1990). 7
Table 2 Description of the samples. Percentages. Base = all respondents. 13
Table 3 Participation in courses now and during the last 3 years. Percentages. Base = all respondents. 15
Table 4 Percentage of all respondents who had participated in different kinds of courses during the last 3 years. Base =all respondents. 16
Table 5 Percentage of participants who had taken 1, 2, 3, 4, 5 or 6 or more courses during the last 3 years. Base = all participants in each type of course. 17
Table 6 Percentage participation in courses during the last 3 years. Base = all respondents in each category. 18
Table 7 Percentage participation in different types of courses during the last 3 years, grouped by gender, age, level of education and employment status. Base = all respondents in each category. 18
Table 8 Information about the most recent course. Base = all participants in courses. 22
Table 9 Proportion of employed participants who have participated in courses during work hours. 23
Table 10 Psychological factors and items defining each factor. 24
Table 11 Percentage of respondents with high, medium and low self-confidence, intrinsic interest value of learning and extrinsic utility value of learning. Base = all respondents. 25
Table 12 Percentage participation in courses during the last 3 years within groups with high, medium and low self-confidence, intrinsic interest value of learning and extrinsic utility value of learning. 25
Table 13 Most important and second most important reason for participating in the most recent course. Base = all participants in courses during the last 3 years. 27
Table 14 Reasons for participation (factor analysis, Norway). 28
Table 15 Distribution of categories of main reasons for participating. Base = all participants in courses. 29
Table 16 Percentage who consider it as "very likely " or "likely" that they will take courses the next 3 years. Base = all respondents. 31
Table 17 Percentage of respondents who consider it "likely" or "very likely" that they will do courses the next 3 years, by participation in courses the last 3-years. Base = all respondents. 32
Table 18 Percentage of employed respondents who are able to get time off from work to follow courses and percentage who consider it likely they would get paid or unpaid leave. Base = all employed. 34
Table 19 Percentage of employed respondents (total and by participation during the last 3 years) who are able to get time off from work to follow courses and percentage

	who consider it likely that they will obtain paid or unpaid leave. Base = all employed.	35
Table 20	Usefulness of most recent course. Percentage of participants who responded "very useful "or "useful" to the given statements. Base = all participants who had completed a course during the last 3 years.	37
Table 21	Main reason and second most important reason for not participating in courses during the last 3 years. Base = all non-participants.	41
Table 22	Categories of barriers (factor analysis of Norwegian data)	42
Table 23	Main barrier factors. Percentage of respondents who indicate each of the factors as the main barrier factor. Base = all non-participants in courses.	43
Table 24	Percentage who prefer different strategies for learning different topics. Base = all respondents.	49
Table 25	Percentage of the respondents who prefer to go to a class in order to learn different topics, grouped by familiarity with the topic.	51
Table 26a	Percentage in different subgroups who prefer to go to a class in order to learn in different areas. Base = all respondents who say they have little or very little knowledge on each area.	51
Table 26b	Percentage in different subgroups who prefer to go to a class in order to learn in different areas. Base = all respondents who say they have little or very little knowledge on each area.	52

APPENDIX

Appendix 1a. The Questionnaire

BACKGROUND VARIABLES

01. Gender: ( ) male ( ) female

02. Age: (__)

03. Level of education:
    - ( ) No formal qualifications
    - ( ) Primary school diploma and lower secondary school diploma (*corresponding with ISCED 1-2*)
    - ( ) Upper secondary school diploma (*corresponding with ISCED 3 and 5*)
    - ( ) College/university degree (*corresponding with ISCED 6-7*)
    - ( ) Other

04. Town/city size:
    - ( ) less than 200 inhabitants
    - ( ) 200 - 1 999 inhabitants
    - ( ) 2 000 - 19 999 inhabitants
    - ( ) 20 000 - 99 999 inhabitants
    - ( ) 100 000 - 199 000 inhabitants
    - ( ) 200 000 - 499 000 inhabitants
    - ( ) 500 000 or more inhabitants

05. Size of household (number of persons in household): (__)

06. Employment.
    Counted as employed are those who usually work for income of at least 10 hours duration per week. As work for income we also mean work performed as a family member without fixed wages at farms, in shops or other family owned businesses.
    What is your work situation currently?
    - ( ) Self-employed
    - ( ) Employed
    - ( ) Unemployed who are looking for the first employment
    - ( ) Unemployed with a labour experience
    - ( ) Retired / at social welfare programs
    - ( ) House-working
    - ( ) Student
    - ( ) Other situations

Question 07 are for those who are employed at the moment.
Others skips to 08.

07. What kind of contract (agreement) do you have?
    - ( ) Permanent
    - ( ) Temporary

08. Weekly working hours (includes main occupation and secondary occupation if applicable, paid overtime and extra work at home in connection to work):
    - ( ) 10-19 hours
    - ( ) 20-34 hours
    - ( ) 35-44 hours
    - ( ) 45 hours or more

09. Personal Gross income during last year:
   ( )   0 - 11 999 Euro)
   ( ) 12 000 - 17 999 Euro)
   ( ) 18 000 - 23 999 Euro)
   ( ) 24 000 - 29 999 Euro)
   ( ) 30 000 - 35 999 Euro)
   ( ) 36 000 - 47 999 Euro)
   ( ) 48 000 - 59 999 Euro)
   ( ) 60 000 - and more Euro)

10. Gross income of household during last year:
   ( )   0 - 11 999 Euro)
   ( ) 12 000 - 17 999 Euro)
   ( ) 18 000 - 23 999 Euro)
   ( ) 24 000 - 29 999 Euro)
   ( ) 30 000 - 35 999 Euro)
   ( ) 36 000 - 47 999 Euro)
   ( ) 48 000 - 59 999 Euro)
   ( ) 60 000 - and more Euro)

ABOUT YOUR EDUCATION DURING THE LAST THREE YEARS

YOU WILL NOW BE ASKED A NUMBER OF QUESTIONS ABOUT EDUCATION AND TRAINING YOU HAVE FOLLOWED DURING THE LAST THREE YEARS. PLEASE NOTE TWO IMPORTANT POINTS:

1) BY EDUCATION AND TRAINING IN THIS CONTEXT WE INCLUDE FORMAL EDUCATION AS WELL AS SHORT COURSES AND OTHER SYSTEMATIC EDUCATIONAL ACTIVITIES WHICH REQUIRE SOME KIND OF INSTRUCTION OR SUPERVISION. THIS ALSO INCLUDES DISTANCE LEARNING, WHICH YOU CAN DO AT HOME.
FROM NOW ON WE WILL USE THE TERM COURSE OR COURSES.

2) AN EDUCATION AND TRAINING PROGRAMME WHICH COMPRISE A NUMBER OF SUBJECTS SHOULD BE CONSIDERED AS ONE COURSE.

11. Are you doing any course(s) at the moment?
   ( ) Yes
   ( ) No

12. Have you followed any courses during the last three years?
   ( ) Yes
   ( ) No

If no to question 11 and question 12, skip to question 26.

13. How many courses have you taken the last three years of the following types:

   a) General and/or academic courses   (__)
   b) Vocational and/or work related courses[1]   (__)
   c) Recreational and leisure courses   (__)
   d) Other courses   (__)

WE SHALL NOW ASK SOME QUESTIONS ABOUT THE LAST COURSE YOU HAVE DONE, WHETHER OR NOT YOU COMPLETED IT. IF YOU ARE DOING A COURSE AT THE MOMENT, COUNT THIS COURSE AS THE LAST ONE. IF YOU ARE DOING SEVERAL COURSES AT THE MOMENT, PLEASE CHOOSE THE ONE YOU HAVE DONE FOR THE LONGEST PERIOD OF TIME.

---

[1] With vocational is here meant all courses you find relevant for your currently or future situation

14. What type of course was the last one you took during the last three years? (State the type of course)
   ( ) General and/or academic course
   ( ) Vocational and/or work related course
   ( ) Recreational and leisure course
   ( ) Other type

15. Have you completed this course?
   ( ) Yes, I have completed it
   ( ) No, I left before I completed it
   ( ) The course is not finished yet

16. How long has/will the course last?
   ( ) Less than 1 week
   ( ) 1 week – 4 weeks
   ( ) 1 - 3 months
   ( ) 4 - 6 months
   ( ) 7 - 12 months
   ( ) Over 1 - 2 years
   ( ) More than 2 years

17. Approximately how many hours per week do/did you spend on this course, including travel, attendance and homework? (___) hours

18. Does/did this course offer accreditation or certification?
   ( ) Yes
   ( ) No

REASONS FOR PARTICIPATING

19. This card lists some reasons people give for choosing to continue your education or take courses. Considering the last course you took, what was the main reason for doing this course ? [show card] ( )
   a) To get a job
   b) To get a job with another employer
   c) To get a (recognised) qualification[2]
   d) To change the type of work I do
   e) To be promoted
   f) To perform my work better
   g) To help me get on a future course.
   h) To develop myself as a person
   i) To improve my self-confidence
   j) I enjoy reading and learning
   k) I am interested in the subject or topic
   l) To meet (new) people
   m) To have something to do
   n) I had no choice – my employer decided / benefit requirement
   o) Other reasons

20. Which of the reasons would you say was the second most important for you? [show card] ( )

21. Which formal qualifications do/did you aim to attain through this course?
   ( ) No formal qualifications
   ( ) Primary school diploma or lower secondary school diploma
       (corresponding with ISCED 1-2)
   ( ) Upper secondary school diploma *(corresponding with ISCED 3 and 5)*
   ( ) College/university degree *(corresponding with ISCED 6-7)*
   ( ) Other

---

[2] The statement in Great Britain emphasised "a recognised qualification" whereas the term recognised was not included in the Norwegian and Spanish questionnaire (question 19, 25 and 40).

22. Who arranges/arranged the course?
    ( ) employer
    ( ) school/college/university
    ( ) adult education centre
    ( ) trade union
    ( ) private providers
    ( ) social or voluntary organisation
    ( ) other

Question 23-24 is only for those who are self employed or employed according to question 06. Others skips to question 25.

23. Are you following/did you follow the course <u>during work hours</u>?
    ( ) Yes
    ( ) No

If yes to question 23, go to question 24. If no, skip to 25.

24. Are you receiving/did you receive full pay while you follow/followed the course?
    ( ) Yes
    ( ) No

USEFULNESS
This is for those who answered no to question 11 and yes to question 12, i.e. those who have completed the course during the last three years and who are not taking any course now. Others go to question 28.

25. How <u>useful</u> was the course you took. I'll now mention different areas for you. How will you consider the usefulness of the course for each of these areas [show card]. Will you say the course was very useful, useful, not very useful or not useful at all?

	Very useful	Useful	Not very useful	Not useful at all
a) To get a job				
b) To get a job with another employer				
c) To get a (recognised) qualification				
d) To change the type of work I do				
e) To be promoted				
f) To perform my work better				
g) To help me on a future course				
h) To develop myself as a person				
i) To improve my self-confidence				
j) I really enjoyed reading and learning				
k) My interest in the subject or topic was stimulated				
l) To meet (new) people				
m) To have something to do				

REASONS FOR NOT TAKING COURSES OR STUDYING NOW
This is for those who answered no to questions 11 and 12, i.e. those who are <u>not doing courses</u> and who <u>have not done so during the last three years</u>. Others go to question 28.

26. This card lists some possible reasons for <u>not pursuing</u> any courses during the last three years. What is <u>the main reason</u> that you have not done any courses the last three years?[Show card] ( )
    a) Too exhausting
    b) Did not have time
    c) Too expensive
    d) Too far to travel
    e) There was no suitable course
    f) Care obligations

g) Difficult getting time off work
h) Found it hard to leave my job
i) Health reasons/feeling too old
j) Not interested
k) Did not have the required qualifications/knowledge
l) Requirements for reading and writing skills too tough
m) Lacked the necessary skills/abilities
n) Did not believe I could manage
o) Felt no need to learn more
p) Did not want to be in a group with people I did not know
q) Worried about going out alone
r) My family did not want me to
s) Language difficulties

27. Which of the reasons would you say is the second most important reason for not participating? [show card] ( )

POSSIBILITIES OF TAKING COURSES DURING WORKING HOURS

Question 28-36 is only for those who are employed according to question 06.
Others skips to question 37.

YOU WILL NOW BE ASKED SOME QUESTIONS ON TAKING COURSES DURING WORKING HOURS.

28. Are you currently in the situation where you are able to get time off from work for education or training?
    ( ) yes
    ( ) no

29. Would you wish to do courses within regular working hours?
    ( ) yes
    ( ) no

30. Would you wish to do courses within regular working hours if you got paid leave (paid time off)?
    ( ) yes
    ( ) no

31. Would you wish to do courses within regular working hours if you got unpaid leave (unpaid time off)?
    ( ) yes
    ( ) no

32. How likely is your employer to give you paid leave for courses within regular working hours?
    ( ) very likely
    ( ) fairly likely
    ( ) not very likely
    ( ) not at all likely

33. How likely is your employer to give you unpaid leave for courses within regular working hours?
    ( ) very likely
    ( ) fairly likely
    ( ) not very likely
    ( ) not at all likely

34. For how long would you consider taking paid leave to do a course you think is really important? (State number of weeks.) (__)

35. For how long would you consider taking unpaid leave to do a course you think is really important? (State number of weeks.) (__)

36. Would it be financially possible for you to take unpaid leave for this period?
    ( ) yes
    ( ) no

For everyone:

FUTURE PLANS FOR TAKING COURSES

WE SHALL NOW ASK YOU SOME QUESTIONS REGARDING <u>FUTURE PLANS</u> FOR TAKING EDUCATION OR TRAINING.

37. How is the <u>ease of access</u> to courses close to where you live?
    ( ) very good
    ( ) good
    ( ) poor
    ( ) very poor

38. How <u>likely</u> is it that you will start at a new course during the next three years?
    ( ) very likely
    ( ) fairly likely
    ( ) not very likely
    ( ) not at all likely

If answer to question 38 is <u>not very likely</u> or <u>not at all likely</u>, skip to 41.

39. I'll now mention four types of courses for you. How likely is it that you will take each of these types of courses during the next three years? Would you say it's very likely, fairly likely, not very likely or not at all likely?

TYPE OF COURSE	Very likely	Fairly likely	Not very likely	Not at all likely
a) General and/or academic course				
b) Vocational and/or work related course				
c) Recreational and leisure course				
d) Other courses				

REASONS FOR TAKING COURSES IN THE FUTURE.
Question 40 is for those who answers <u>very likely</u> or <u>fairly likely</u> to question 38.
Others skips to question 41.

40. This card lists some reasons for taking courses. Irrespective of the course you would perhaps like to take, which is the <u>most important reason</u> why you want to pursue more education? [Show card] (_)
    a) To get a job
    b) To get a job with another employer
    c) To get a (recognised) qualification
    d) To change the type of work I do
    e) To be promoted
    f) To perform my work better
    g) To help me get on a future course.
    h) To develop myself as a person
    i) To improve my self-confidence
    j) I enjoy reading and learning
    k) I am interested in the subject or topic
    l) To meet (new) people
    m) To have something to do
    n) I had no choice – my employer decided / benefit requirement
    o) Other reasons

For everyone:

ABOUT LEARNING

41. I'll now mention for you four topics that some people would like to learn more about. How much will you say you know about each of these topics? Will you say you know very much, quite a lot, a little or very little? [Show card]

TOPIC	Very much	Quite a lot	A little	Very Little
a) Cookery				
b) Computers/Electronic data processing				
c) Work related laws and rules				
d) *[English]*[3]				

42. a) Can you name another topic, which you really want to learn more about?
        ( ) yes   ( ) no

If no to question 42a, skip to question 44. If yes to 42a:

    b) What topic is it? (_____)

43. How much would you say you know about this topic?
        ( ) Very much   ( ) Quite a lot   ( ) A little   ( ) Very little

44. If you were to learn more about the former topics, how would you prefer to learn each one? [show card] Will you go to a class, seek information or try it out on your own, ask somebody you know for advice or guidance, watch/listen to TV/radio instruction programmes, take a correspondence course or use Internet/modern technology? Only one answer is possible to each.

	Go to a class	Seek information or try it out on my own	Ask somebody I know for advice or guidance	Watch/listen to TV/radio instruction programmes	Take a corre-spondence course	Use Internet/ modern technology
a) Cookery						
b) Computers/Electronic data processing						
c) Work related laws and rules						
d) *[English]*[4]						
e) Other topic that you say you really want to learn about[5]						

---

[3] *For the UK and Spain: First/most important foreign language at school*
[4] *For the UK and Spain: First/most important foreign language at school*
[5] *Only for those who answered yes to question 42a*

45. I shall now read some statements to you. To what extent do you agree that each statement fits you? Alternatives are on this card. [Show card]. Will you say you agree, partly agree, both agree and disagree or disagree?

	Agree	Partly agree	Both agree and disagree	Partly disagree	Disagree
a) I have always wanted to learn more					
b) Learning something new is fun					
c) I need to improve my knowledge					
d) I always found it easy to learn					
e) I'll need further and continuing education within the next three to five years					
f) If I should do a course or learn more it must be because the content of the course is interesting					
g) I know I can manage any education if I set my mind to it					
h) I have always felt comfortable in school-like situations					
i) If I should participate in education or training it would be because I think learning in itself is fun					
j) I worry about doing mistakes when I am in a school-like situation					
k) I am a valuable person, at least as valuable as others					
l) If there is something I want to learn, I know that I can do it					
m) I have nothing to gain by further education and training					
n) I am satisfied with myself					
o) I am good at planning my own learning activities					
p) For my own sake I see no purpose in further education and training					

46. Evaluating your ability, would you say you are <u>very able, able or not very able</u> in the following areas:

	Very able	Able	Not very able
a) Drawing and painting	( )	( )	( )
b) Playing an instrument	( )	( )	( )
c) Sports	( )	( )	( )
d) Ability to learn school subjects	( )	( )	( )
e) Reading	( )	( )	( )
f) Writing	( )	( )	( )
g) Mathematics	( )	( )	( )

ABOUT READING AND WRITING DIFFICULTIES

The following questions are for those who answered "not very able" in the areas reading and/or writing in question 46. Others skips to question 49.

AS YOU HAVE ANSWERED THAT <u>YOU ARE NOT VERY ABLE</u> AT READING AND WRITING SKILLS, WE HAVE SOME ADDITIONAL QUESTIONS FOR YOU REGARDING READING AND/OR WRITING DIFFICULTIES.

47. To what extent have reading and/or writing difficulties prevented you from <u>getting the education you wanted or taking courses as an adult</u>?
　　　　( ) A great deal
　　　　( ) To some extent
　　　　( ) Little extent/not at all

48. To what extent have reading and/or writing difficulties prevented you from <u>getting the job you wanted</u>?
　　　　( ) A great deal
　　　　( ) To some extent
　　　　( ) Little extent/not at all

OTHER BACKGROUND VARIABLES

49. How many persons are you <u>caring</u> for? (__)

50. <u>Number of children</u> in household:
　　　　a) under 5 years　　(__)
　　　　b) 5 – 16 years　　　(__)
　　　　c) 16 years and more　(__)

51. Access to <u>telephone</u>:
　　　　( ) not at all
　　　　( ) only at job
　　　　( ) only at home
　　　　( ) both at job and at home
　　　　( ) other places

52. Access to <u>PC:</u>
　　　　( ) not at all
　　　　( ) only at job
　　　　( ) only at home
　　　　( ) both at job and at home
　　　　( ) other places

53. Access to <u>ICT/Internet</u>:
　　　　( ) not at all
　　　　( ) only at job
　　　　( ) only at home
　　　　( ) both at job and at home
　　　　( ) other places

54. Have you in your own opinion experienced any <u>personal crises</u> or other very <u>stressful life events</u> during the last three years?
　　　　( ) yes
　　　　( ) no

Question 55 is for those who answered yes to 54. Others skips to question 56.

55. As you see it, has this <u>prevented</u> you from taking education or courses?
　　　　( ) yes
　　　　( ) no

56. Currently, how will you describe <u>your economic situation</u>?
　　　　( ) low
　　　　( ) below average
　　　　( ) average
　　　　( ) above average
　　　　( ) high

Appendix 1b. Definitions

Household = joint household, that is, persons who share board and lodging

House-working = carrying out unpaid work in the home. It is assumed that the person is not unemployed, is not a pensioner and is not a student

Retired/at social welfare programs = person in receipt of an old age pension, widow's pension or disability pension

Student = someone who is at school or who studies for at least 10 hours per week

General and/or academic course = a course which is not directed towards a given occupation, and which is not connected with hobbies or recreation

Vocational and/or work related course = a course which the respondent feels is of relevance to his/her current or future work

Recreational and leisure course = a course which is connected to recreational or spare time activities and which the respondent defines as a part of his/her own spare time activities.

Unemployed = employed for less than 10 hours per week in the last three months

Temporary employment = has an employment contract of a limited duration. This includes supply posts and contracts.

Adult education centre = institute set up by the local authority to offer adult education.

Private course organiser = e.g. commercial companies/ institutions which offer training and courses in different areas and which offer their services to companies, public departments and individuals.

Voluntary organisations = e.g. idealistic membership organisations, such as environmental protection organisations, parishes, aid organisations and similar groups which offer courses within their own areas of interest.

Working hours = the period when one normally works. For an employee, working hours are defined as the hours which are normally to be worked according to the agreement with the employer. For self-employed and freelance individuals, working hours are defined as the time one normally and on average is employed in paid work.

Caring for = here this is taken to mean caring for others in the form of nursing and help in everyday life. This can include caring for children or nursing elderly and handicapped people who live at home, and who share board and lodging with the respondent. People who are cared for but who do not live in the joint household, are not included. Financial support for care is not included here.

Personal crises or other very stressfull life events = in order for an event to be considered as a personal crisis, it must have been experienced as a crisis by the respondent. Divorce, loss of close family members, accidents which affect an individual or members of the family, and serious mental or physical illnesses are all examples of events which can lead to life crises.

Appendix 2. Factor analysis of self-perception and motivation items

Variable	Factor 1 Self confidence	Factor 2 Intrinsic interest value of learning	Factor 3 Extrinsic utility value of learning
v81s	.772		
v84s	.758		
v82s	.618		
v72s		.809	
v71s		.767	
v79s		.710	
v83			.905
v86			.897

Extraction: Principal Component Analysis
Rotation: Varimax
Note: Only loadings > .400 are included in the table.

Variables:

v81s = I am a valuable person, at least as valuable as others
v84s = I am satisfied with myself
v82s = If there is something I want to learn, I know that I can do it

v72s = Learning something new is fun
v71s = I have always wanted to learn more
v79s = If I should participate in education or training it would be because I think learning in itself is fun

v83 = I have nothing to gain by further education and training
v86 = For my own sake I see no purpose in further education and training

Appendix 3. Participation in courses during the last 3 years within groups with high, medium and low self confidence, intrinsic interest value of learning and extrinsic utility value of learning

Appendix 3a. Per cent participation in courses during the last 3 years within groups with high, medium and low self confidence. Base = all respondents.

		Total			Self confidence								
					High			Medium			Low		
		GB	Nor	Sp	GB	Nor	Sp	GB	Nor	Sp	GB	Nor	Sp
		N=1571	N=1836	N=1920	N=434	N=666	N=537	N=583	N=774	N=567	N=535	N=385	N=795
All respondents		41	70	32	39	74	42	43	71	34	42	61	25
Gender	Men	40	70	31	35	73	39	45	70	34	39	65	24
	Women	43	70	34	43	75	45	42	72	35	43	57	26
Age group	18-29	64	88	64	71	88	71	63	90	62	60	88	59
	30-45	50	76	33	43	77	39	51	77	37	55	69	26
	46-59	42	73	18	44	79	26	42	70	16	41	71	15
	60-79	17	28	7	14	33	7	18	27	8	18	27	5
Level of education	No formal	18	**	7	19	**	14	15	**	8	19	**	4
	Prim/l.sec	45	40	27	37	51	32	48	37	30	46	30	23
	Upper sec	61	72	54	60	76	59	64	72	52	58	68	52
	Col./univ.	65	83	60	70	84	63	66	86	59	61	74	56

** N < 20

Appendix 3b. Per cent participation in courses last 3 years within groups with high, medium and low intrinsic interest value of learning. Base = all respondents.

		Total			Intrinsic interest value of learning								
					High			Medium			Low		
		GB	Nor	Sp	GB	Nor	Sp	GB	Nor	Sp	GB	Nor	Sp
		N=1571	N=1836	N=1920	N=423	N=443	N=424	N=746	N=997	N=697	N=380	N=387	N=784
All respondents		41	70	32	51	69	45	43	73	38	28	63	21
Gender	Men	40	70	31	45	69	42	43	73	40	30	63	20
	Women	43	70	34	55	69	47	43	74	37	27	62	23
Age group	18-29	64	88	64	67	89	75	65	89	66	56	87	56
	30-45	50	76	33	59	74	47	52	79	35	35	69	23
	46-59	42	73	18	48	78	24	39	71	22	41	71	11
	60-79	17	28	7	33	31	14	15	33	14	6	19	1
Level of education	No formal	18	**	7	29	**	14	18	**	12	12	**	2
	Prim/l.sec	45	40	27	52	44	38	46	45	30	32	29	20
	Upper sec	61	72	54	67	69	59	58	75	60	60	70	46
	Col./univ.	65	83	60	69	79	68	68	86	64	48	83	44

** N < 20

Appendix 3c. Per cent participation in courses last 3 years by groups with high, medium and low extrinsic utility value of learning. Base = all respondents.

		Total			Extrinsic utility value of learning								
					High			Medium			Low		
		GB	Nor	Sp	GB	Nor	Sp	GB	Nor	Sp	GB	Nor	Sp
		N=1571	N=1836	N=1920	N=755	N=787	N=593	N=405	N=604	N=801	N=393	N=437	N=520
All respondents		41	70	32	63	85	55	33	72	26	10	40	17
Gender	Men	40	70	31	61	87	57	33	72	23	8	38	17
	Women	43	70	34	64	84	54	33	71	29	11	42	17
Age group	18-29	64	88	64	75	90	78	44	87	51	**	75*	56
	30-45	50	76	33	63	83	48	30	73	25	24	55	26
	46-59	42	73	18	60	85	38	39	74	13	12	58	8
	60-79	17	28	7	46	**	12	22	43	10	4	23	2
Level of education	No formal	18	**	7	42	**	22	19	**	8	5	**	2
	Prim/l.sec	45	40	27	59	63	41	32	52	26	18	18	17
	Upper sec	61	72	54	73	85	74	46	72	34	**	46	44
	Col./univ.	65	83	60	74	93	71	50	82	47	30*	58	42

* Percentage must be interpreted with caution, due to low N (N ≥ 20 and < 30)
** N < 20

Appendix 4. Factor analysis of reasons for participation

Variable	Factor 1 Personal development	Factor 2 New work situation	Factor 3 Carrying out one's work better
v208	.783		
v209	.737		
v210	.717		
v211	.662		
v202		.810	
v201		.682	
v204		.632	
v205		.596	
v206			.899
v203			.690

Extraction: Principal Component Analysis
Rotation: Varimax
Note: Only loadings > .400 are included in the table.

Variables:
v208 = to develop myself as a person
v209 = to improve my self confidence
v210 = I enjoy reading and learning
v211 = I am interested in the subject/topic

v202 = to get a job with another employer
v201 = to get a job
v204 = to change the type of work I do
v205 = to be promoted

v206 = to perform my work better
v203 = to get a (recognised) qualification

Appendix 5. Main reasons for participation in courses

Appendix 5a. Main reasons for participation in courses. Total and by gender. Base = all participants in courses.

	All participants			Men			Women		
	GB	Nor	Sp	GB	Nor	Sp	GB	Nor	Sp
Factors/variables	646	1279	618	276	639	292	370	640	326
Factor 1. Personal development	24	20	20	19	17	14	28	24	25
Factor 2. New work situation	22	15	40	22	14	40	21	16	39
Factor 3. Perform work better	40	49	32	42	54	39	39	45	25
Had no choice	10	8	2	13	9	3	7	6	1
Other reasons	5	8	7	4	7	3	5	9	10
Total	**101**	**100**	**101**	**100**	**101**	**99**	**100**	**100**	**100**

NOTE: total varies from 99 to 101 due to rounding of decimals

Appendix 5b. Main reasons for participation in courses by age groups. Base = all participants in courses.

	18-29			30-45			46-59			60-79		
	GB	Nor	Sp	GB	Nor	Sp	GB	Nor	Sp	GB	Nor	Sp
Factors/variables	165	389	328	257	495	191	155	302	70	69	93	28*
Factor 1. Personal development	13	24	17	17	15	18	27	19	20	70	37	71*
Factor 2. New work situation	35	27	51	24	12	34	11	7	16	4	2	0
Factor 3. Perform work better	44	35	25	44	58	40	43	58	50	16	40	11*
Had no choice	2	6	1	13	7	3	15	11	6	6	7	0
Other reasons	7	9	6	3	8	5	5	6	9	4	15	18*
Total	**101**	**101**	**100**	**101**	**100**	**100**	**101**	**101**	**101**	**100**	**101**	**100**

NOTE: total varies from 100 to 101 due to rounding of decimals
* Percentage must be interpreted with caution, due to low N (N ≥ 20 and < 30)

Appendix 5c. Main reasons for participation in courses by level of education. Base = all participants in courses.

	No formal			Primary/lower secondary			Upper secondary			College/ university		
	GB	Nor	Sp	GB	Nor	Sp	GB	Nor	Sp	GB	Nor	Sp
Factors/variables	94	0	21*	165	115	269	112	724	179	229	421	134
Factor 1. Personal development	35	-	38*	23	27	22	21	18	21	22	22	13
Factor 2. New work situation	18	-	24*	21	17	40	29	17	40	22	9	40
Factor 3. Perform work better	27	-	29*	41	37	27	39	49	33	46	55	41
Had no choice	14	-	0	10	5	3	6	8	1	6	7	3
Other reasons	6	-	10*	4	15	9	5	8	5	4	7	4
Total	**100**	**-**	**101**	**99**	**101**	**101**	**100**	**100**	**100**	**100**	**100**	**101**

NOTE: total varies from 99 to 101 due to rounding of decimals
* Percentage must be interpreted with caution, due to low N (N ≥ 20 and < 30)

Appendix 5d. Main reasons for participation in courses by type of course. Base = all participants in courses.

	General and academic			Vocational			Recreational and leisure		
	GB	Nor	Sp	GB	Nor	Sp	GB	Nor	Sp
Factors/variables	169	99	265	386	985	244	82	133	71
Factor 1. Personal development	33	21	19	7	13	8	81	65	65
Factor 2. New work situation	31	24	55	21	15	30	4	4	13
Factor 3. Perform work better	30	33	18	53	58	56	5	11	7
Had no choice	1	0	1	15	9	4	1	2	0
Other reasons	5	21	8	4	5	2	10	19	16
Total	**100**	**99**	**101**	**100**	**100**	**100**	**101**	**101**	**101**

NOTE: total varies from 99 to 101 due to rounding of decimals

Appendix 6. Path analyses predicting likelihood of participation next three years

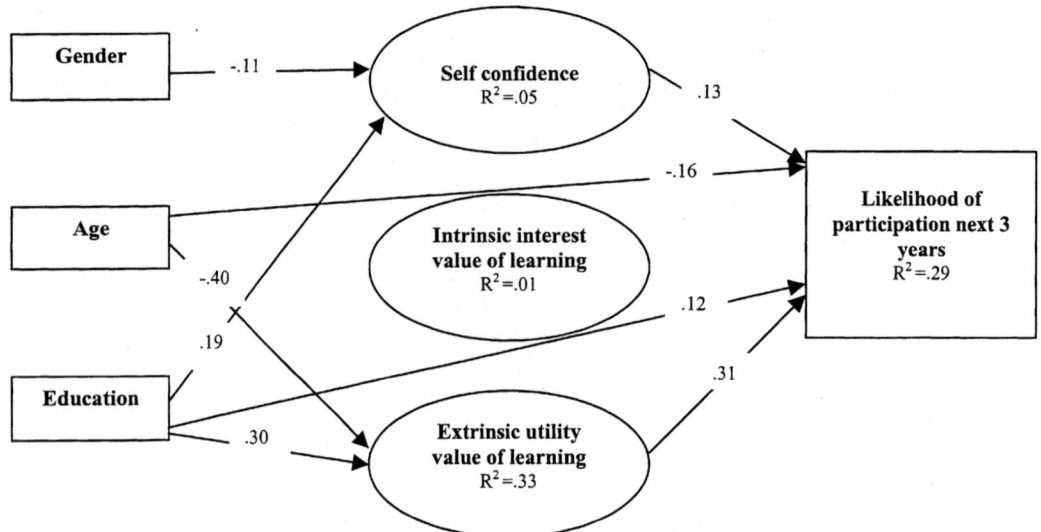

Note: Beta values below .10 are not included in the figure.

Appendix 6a.   Great Britain.

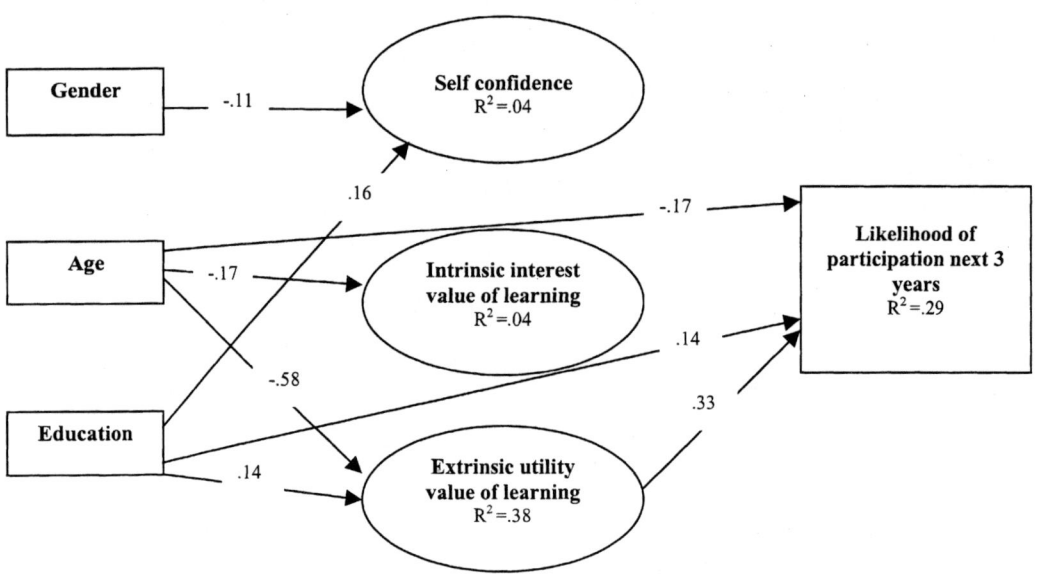

Note: Beta values below .10 are not included in the figure.

Appendix 6b.   Norway.

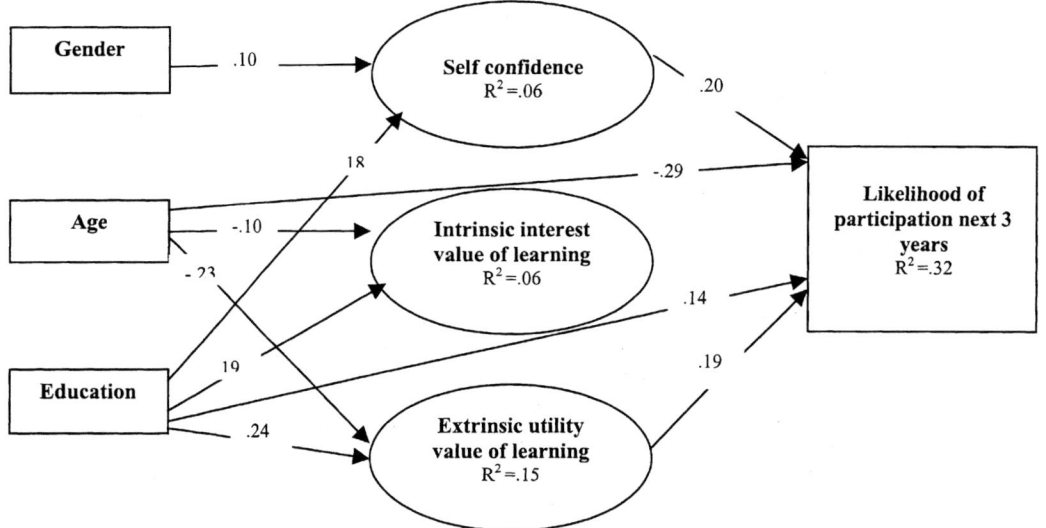

Note: Beta values below .10 are not included in the figure.

Appendix 6c. Spain.

Appendix 7. Per cent of employed respondents who are able to get time off from work to follow courses and per cent who consider it likely to get paid or unpaid leave

Appendix 7a. Total results and results by gender. Base = all employed.

	Total			Men			Women		
	GB	Nor	Sp	GB	Nor	Sp	GB	Nor	Sp
	811	1266	815	415	691	536	397	581	287
Able to get time off from work	57	67	28	58	69	27	56	64	29
Likelihood getting paid leave	49	63	24	49	65	25	50	60	21
Likelihood getting unpaid leave	40	63	24	39	61	25	41	66	22

Appendix 7b. Results for different age groups. Base = all employed.

	18-29			30-45			46-59			60-79		
	GB	Nor	Sp	GB	Nor	Sp	GB	Nor	Sp	GB	Nor	Sp
	167	283	236	360	576	357	231	346	205	54	67	23*
Able to get time off from work	59	63	34	58	68	28	55	68	24	50	64	9*
Likelihood getting paid leave	47	55	25	50	66	26	50	66	20	51	50	17*
Likelihood getting unpaid leave	48	64	26	39	65	26	37	62	19	31	52	17*

* Percentage must be interpreted with caution, due to low N (N ≥ 20 and < 30)

Appendix 7c. Results by level of education. Base = all employed.

	No formal			Primary/lower sec			Upper second			College/univ		
	GB	Nor	Sp	GB	Nor	Sp	GB	Nor	Sp	GB	Nor	Sp
	159	0	68	213	114	443	121	720	154	262	417	140
Able to get time off from work	42	-	13	48	58	21	55	65	38	76	72	47
Likelihood getting paid leave	37	-	13	43	54	18	53	60	32	61	71	40
Likelihood getting unpaid leave	34	-	9	37	58	18	38	62	30	49	67	41

Appendix 8. Factor analysis of statements of usefulness of the last course

Variable	Factor 1 Personal development	Factor 2 New work situation	Factor 3 Carrying out one's work better
v35	.815		
v36	.804		
v37	.748		
v38	.578		
v29		.819	
v28		.760	
v32		.625	
v31		.548	
v33			.842
v30			.800

Extraction: Principal Component Analysis
Rotation: Varimax
Note: Only loadings > .400 are included in the table.

Variables:

v35 = to develop myself as a person
v36 = to improve my self confidence
v37 = I enjoy reading and learning
v38 = I was interested in the subject/topic

v29 = to get a job with another employer
v28 = to get a job
v32 = to be promoted
v31 = to change the type of work I do

v33 = to perform my work better
v30 = to get a (recognised) qualification

Appendix 9. Perceived usefulness of the last course

Appendix 9a. Usefulness of last course. Per cent of <u>men and women</u> who responded "very useful" or "useful" to the given statements. Base = all participants who had completed a course during the last 3 years.

	Total			Great Britain		Norway		Spain	
	GB	Nor	Sp	Men	Wom	Men	Wom	Men	Wom
The course was useful	N=304	N=967	N=340	N=149	N=155	N=515	N=452	N=167	N=173
Personal development:									
to develop myself as a person	80	44	91	79	81	39	50	92	90
to improve my self-confidence	76	38	81	75	76	31	44	81	81
I really enjoyed reading and learning	54	41	71	51	57	34	49	69	72
my interest in the subject or topic was stimulated	81	79	86	78	84	76	83	86	86
New work situation:									
to get a job with another employer	38	16	24	40	37	18	14	23	24
to get a job	48	22	45	48	48	22	23	43	47
to change the type of work I do	38	24	29	39	37	24	23	26	32
to be promoted	35	9	48	36	35	11	7	51	44
Perform work better:									
to get a (recognised) qualification	53	76	83	56	51	78	74	86	80
to perform my work better	74	68	73	80	68	70	67	80	67
Other:									
to help me get on a future course	50	35	63	48	52	31	39	62	63
to meet (new) people	59	34	72	57	61	31	38	65	79
to have something to do	56	11	68	55	57	9	13	65	70

Appendix 9b. Usefulness of last course. Per cent within different <u>age groups</u> who responded "very useful" or "useful" to the given statements. Base = all participants who had completed a course during the last 3 years.

	18-29			30-45			46-59			60-79		
	GB	Nor	Sp	GB	Nor	Sp	GB	Nor	Sp	GB	Nor	Sp
The course was useful	N=56	N=229	N=140	N=125	N=399	N=138	N=91	N=259	N=48	N=32	N=80	N=13**
Personal development:												
to develop myself as a person	93	52	91	78	46	90	78	39	90	72	33	**
to improve my self-confidence	82	45	83	74	37	80	75	33	71	72	31	**
I really enjoyed reading and learning	63	39	71	50	40	66	53	42	80	55	48	**
my interest in the subject or topic was stimulated	75	79	85	85	81	85	81	75	86	75	83	**
New work situation:												
to get a job with another employer	42	22	29	44	19	25	33	10	13	25	3	**
to get a job	61	37	53	54	22	46	32	16	27	47	5	**
to change the type of work I do	42	28	31	46	23	36	31	24	12	19	14	**
to be promoted	42	14	45	41	10	52	29	6	45	19	4	**
Perform work better:												
to get a (recognised) qualification	70	73	87	57	82	83	47	74	82	28	65	**
to perform my work better	76	61	70	88	73	77	65	73	77	38	48	**
Other:												
to help me get on a future course	56	44	63	54	36	63	45	30	69	34	18	**
to meet (new) people	70	37	77	57	33	71	57	31	57	56	40	**
to have something to do	64	19	71	48	8	65	58	5	59	66	19	**

** N < 20

Appendix 9c. Usefulness of, last course. Per cent within different <u>educational groups</u> who responded "very useful "or "useful" to the given statements. Base = all participants who had completed a course during the last 3 years.

	No formal			Primary or lower secondary school			Upper secondary school			College/ university		
	GB	Nor	Sp	GB	Nor	Sp	GB	Nor	Sp	GB	Nor	Sp
The course was useful	N=45	N=0	N=11**	N=76	N=87	N=163	N=48	N=551	N=78	N=105	N=317	N=79
Personal development:												
to develop myself as a person	78	-	**	84	47	93	76	45	91	82	42	85
to improve my self-confidence	76	-	**	75	44	87	74	42	78	76	29	71
I really enjoyed reading and learning	58	-	**	57	45	74	45	40	66	55	41	71
my interest in the subject or topic was stimulated	82	-	**	82	76	87	67	79	86	86	81	81
New work situation:												
to get a job with another employer	31	-	**	43	16	22	34	19	23	41	11	27
to get a job	42	-	**	55	26	44	40	25	48	53	16	41
to change the type of work I do	31	-	**	51	20	30	40	27	20	34	19	35
to be promoted	18	-	**	32	9	46	23	10	47	52	7	48
Perform work better:												
to get a (recognised) qualification	44	-	**	68	67	81	51	79	84	48	76	86
to perform my work better	53	-	**	75	58	69	77	69	75	82	70	80
Other:												
to help me get on a future course	47	-	**	61	43	58	42	38	68	49	27	65
to meet (new) people	69	-	**	55	44	77	47	35	70	61	31	62
to have something to do	67	-	**	61	23	77	47	12	58	52	5	53

** N < 20

Appendix 9d. Usefulness of last course. Per cent of participants within different <u>types of courses</u> who responded "very useful "or "useful" to the given statements. Base = all participants who had completed a course during the last 3 years.

	General and academic course			Vocational course			Recreational and leisure course		
	GB	Nor	Sp	GB	Nor	Sp	GB	Nor	Sp
The course was useful	N=56	N=46	N=102	N=211	N=768	N=180	N=35	N=105	N=31
Personal development:									
to develop myself as a person	84	48	91	81	42	90	69	51	100
to improve my self-confidence	80	41	87	75	36	76	69	41	84
I really enjoyed reading and learning	71	48	80	49	39	65	54	47	74
my interest in the subject or topic was stimulated	89	65	86	79	79	84	83	88	94
New work situation:									
to get a job with another employer	41	15	32	42	18	22	11	5	7
to get a job	56	37	47	51	24	47	17	11	19
to change the type of work I do	31	22	37	43	27	29	17	3	7
to be promoted	30	15	40	41	10	59	11	2	16
Perform work better:									
to get a (recognised) qualification	64	70	85	54	83	88	31	42	45
to perform my work better	60	41	61	86	78	89	23	16	36
Other:									
to help me get on a future course	61	54	68	52	34	67	17	28	29
to meet (new) people	73	39	85	56	29	62	60	65	97
to have something to do	73	22	80	48	7	56	77	32	87

Appendix 10. Factor analysis of responses to barrier statements

Variable	Factor 1 Low mastery expectations	Factor 2 Social insecurity	Factor 3 Work commitments	Factor 4 Lack of energy	Factor 5 Lack of time	Factor 6 Lack of motivation
v229	.823					
v230	.786					
v228	.759					
v227	.646					
v235	.518	.401				
v233		.810				
v232		.720				
v234		.660				
v224			.899			
v223			.889			
v217				.772		
v225				.753		
v220				.458		
v222					.848	
v218			-.428		.665	
v231						.839
v226						.813

Extraction: Principal Component Analysis
Rotation: Varimax
Note: Only loadings > .400 are included in the table.

Variables:

v229 = Lacked the necessary skills/abilities
v230 = Did not believe I could manage
v228 = Requirements for reading and writing skills too tough
v227 = Did not have the required qualifications
v235 = Language difficulties

v233 = Worried about going out alone
v232 = Did not want to be in a group with people I did not know
v234 = My family did not want me to

v224 = Found it hard to leave my job
v223 = Difficult getting time off work

v217 = Too exhausting
v225 = Health reasons/feeling too old
v220 = Too far to travel

v222 = Care obligations
v218 = Did not have time

v231 = Felt no need to learn more
v226 = Not interested

Appendix 11. Distribution of main barrier factors on subgroups of respondents

Appendix 11a. Main barrier factors by gender. Per cent of respondents who points at each of the factors as the main barrier factor. Base = all non-participants in courses.

	Great Britain		Norway		Spain	
	Men	Wom	Men	Wom	Men	Wom
Barrier factors and barrier variables	N= 412	N= 496	N= 272	N= 270	N= 653	N= 638
Low mastery expectations	2	4	2	4	5	4
Social insecurity	0	2	0	2	0	0
Work commitments	8	2	6	3	9	4
Lack of energy	16	16	20	27	18	14
Lack of time	25	39	21	26	45	56
Lack of motivation	40	29	33	22	19	16
High costs	3	4	4	7	1	2
No suitable course	5	4	15	10	4	4
Total	99	100	101	101	101	100

NOTE: total varies from 99 to 101 due to rounding of decimals

Appendix 11b. Main barrier factors by age groups. Per cent of respondents who points at each of the factors as the main barrier factor. Base = all non-participants in courses.

	18-29			30-45			46-59			60-79		
	GB	No	Sp	GB	No	Sp	GB	No	Sp	GB	No	Sp
Barrier factors and barrier variables	N= 92	N= 46	N= 185	N= 257	N= 153	N= 381	N= 214	N= 107	N= 329	N= 345	N= 236	N= 394
Low mastery expectations	3	4	2	4	1	2	3	4	4	3	3	9
Social insecurity	1	0	0	0	1	0	1	2	0	2	1	0
Work commitments	10	7	11	7	7	9	6	7	8	1	1	2
Lack of energy	2	4	5	10	13	8	20	24	12	22	34	32
Lack of time	57	44	62	47	39	65	33	20	56	15	11	26
Lack of motivation	19	17	15	23	16	10	28	21	16	50	40	27
High costs	7	7	2	5	9	2	4	6	2	2	2	1
No suitable course	2	17	5	5	14	5	5	18	3	5	8	3
Total	101	100	102	101	100	101	100	102	101	100	100	100

NOTE: total varies from 100 to 102 due to rounding of decimals

Appendix 11c. Main barrier factors by level of education. Per cent of respondents who points at each of the factors as the main barrier factor. Base = all non-participants in courses.

	No formal			Primary or lower secondary			Upper secondary			College/ university		
	GB	No	Sp	GB	No	Sp	GB	No	Sp	GB	No	Sp
Barrier factors and barrier variables	N= 438	N= 0	N= 294	N= 204	N= 172	N= 723	N= 72	N= 270	N= 150	N= 121	N= 85	N= 89
Low mastery expectations	5	-	9	3	6	4	0	2	0	0	0	5
Social insecurity	2	-	0	1	1	0	0	1	0	1	1	0
Work commitments	4	-	4	6	2	6	7	7	11	5	2	11
Lack of energy	22	-	26	8	31	13	11	21	12	11	18	11
Lack of time	24	-	35	43	15	54	36	26	61	46	31	54
Lack of motivation	37	-	23	29	35	17	32	23	12	26	27	12
High costs	3	-	1	5	4	2	4	5	1	2	8	0
No suitable course	3	-	1	3	8	4	10	15	2	10	13	7
Total	100	-	99	98	102	100	100	100	99	101	100	100

NOTE: total varies from 98 to 102 due to rounding of decimals

Appendix 11d. Main barrier factors by <u>employment status</u>. Per cent of respondents who points at each of the factors as the main barrier factor. Base = all non-participants in courses.

Barrier factors and barrier variables	Employed			Unemployed			Not seeking work			Retired		
	GB	No	Sp	GB	No	Sp	GB	No	Sp	GB	No	Sp
	N = 404	N = 252	N = 526	N = 23*	N = 9**	N = 94	N = 175	N = 34	N = 344	N = 282	N = 232	N = 313
Low mastery expectations	3	1	1	13*	**	7	5	3	5	3	4	8
Social insecurity	0	0	0	0*	**	0	2	0	0	3	2	0
Work commitments	10	9	15	13*	**	2	1	0	0	0	0	2
Lack of energy	6	11	6	0*	**	11	31	27	13	24	38	38
Lack of time	43	36	65	30*	**	47	38	35	57	13	7	19
Lack of motivation	30	19	10	13*	**	20	20	24	18	50	39	29
High costs	4	7	1	22*	**	3	2	3	3	2	3	0
No suitable course	5	18	3	9*	**	10	1	9	3	5	7	4
Total	**101**	**101**	**101**	**100**	****	**100**	**100**	**101**	**99**	**100**	**100**	**100**

NOTE: total varies from 99 to 101 due to rounding of decimals
* Percentage must be interpreted with caution, due to low N (N ≥ 20 and < 30)
** N < 20

Appendix 12. Main barrier factors by self perception and motivation

Appendix 12a. Main barrier factors by perceived self-confidence. Per cent of respondents who points at each of the factors as the main barrier factor. Base = all non-participants.

	Self–confidence								
	High			Medium			Low		
	GB	No	Sp	GB	No	Sp	GB	No	Sp
Barrier factors	N= 263	N= 168	N= 310	N= 328	N= 219	N= 370	N= 311	N= 149	N= 596
Low mastery expectations	2	4	3	4	2	5	4	3	5
Social insecurity	1	1	0	1	0	0	2	3	0
Work commitments	4	4	7	5	5	6	6	3	7
Lack of energy	16	17	11	15	25	17	17	28	18
Lack of time	32	29	57	31	23	54	34	19	45
Lack of motivation	37	27	14	37	28	13	29	28	22
High costs	3	5	1	4	5	1	4	7	2
No suitable course	5	14	6	4	13	4	5	9	2
Total	100	101	99	101	101	100	101	100	101

NOTE: total varies from 99 to 101 due to rounding of decimals

Appendix 12b. Main barrier factors by intrinsic interest value of learning. Per cent of respondents who points at each of the factors as the main barrier factor. Base = all non-participants in courses.

	Intrinsic interest value of learning								
	High			Medium			Low		
	GB	No	Sp	GB	No	Sp	GB	No	Sp
Barrier factors	N= 207	N= 134	N= 232	N= 423	N= 260	N= 429	N= 269	N= 142	N= 615
Low mastery expectations	5	3	3	3	3	4	3	3	5
Social insecurity	2	0	0	1	1	0	2	2	0
Work commitments	6	2	5	4	6	6	5	4	8
Lack of energy	17	25	13	14	23	13	17	22	20
Lack of time	38	30	61	36	26	58	23	14	41
Lack of motivation	23	16	12	33	26	14	45	42	22
High costs	3	8	2	5	5	2	2	3	1
No suitable course	7	16	5	5	11	3	2	11	3
Total	101	100	101	101	101	100	99	101	100

NOTE: total varies from 99 to 101 due to rounding of decimals

Appendix 12c. Main barrier factors by extrinsic utility value of learning. Per cent of respondents who points at each of the factors as the main barrier factor. Base = all non-participants in courses.

	Extrinsic utility value of learning								
	High			Medium			Low		
	GB	No	Sp	GB	No	Sp	GB	No	Sp
Barrier factors	N= 278	N= 112	N= 263	N= 271	N= 168	N= 593	N= 352	N= 257	N= 430
Low mastery expectations	3	3	3	4	2	3	3	3	7
Social insecurity	1	1	0	0	1	0	3	1	0
Work commitments	8	5	11	5	7	7	2	2	4
Lack of energy	7	12	10	14	19	14	25	31	22
Lack of time	52	41	58	34	30	56	15	12	39
Lack of motivation	17	14	11	34	20	15	49	39	24
High costs	7	9	1	3	7	2	2	3	1
No suitable course	5	15	8	7	15	3	2	9	4
Total	100	100	102	101	101	100	101	100	101

NOTE: total varies from 100 to 102 due to rounding of decimals